ECONOMICS OF ENTERTAINMENT

THE ECONOMICS OF A ROCK CONCERT

Sheri Perl

Crabtree Publishing Company

www.crabtreebooks.com

Author: Sheri Perl
Editor-in-chief: Lionel Bender
Editors: Simon Adams, Rachel Eagen
Proofreaders: Laura Booth, Wendy Scavuzzo
Project coordinator: Kathy Middleton
Design and photo research: Ben White
Cover design: Margaret Amy Salter
Production: Kim Richardson
Print and production coordinator:
    Margaret Amy Salter
Prepress technician: Margaret Amy Salter

Consultant: Laura Ebert, Ph.D., Lecturer in Economics at the State University of New York at New Paltz, N.Y.

This book was produced for Crabtree Publishing Company by Bender Richardson White.

Photographs and reproductions:
Getty Images: 14–15 (Digital Vision), 22–23 (AFP), 26–27 (AFP), 28–29 (Rick Diamond), 32–33 (Bryan Bedder). Shutterstock.com: cover-top (dwphotos), cover-center (Keith Tarrier), cover-top right insets (Sergii Korolko), cover-bottom right inset (Susan Quinland-Stringer), cover-bottom left inset (Alexey Laputin), banners (Goran Djukanovic), icons (Semisatch, Warren Goldswain, Viorel Sima, Piotr Marcinski, Dario Sabljak, optimarc, Alexander Demyanenko), 1 bottom middle (Randy Miramontez), 4-5 (Randy Miramontez), 6-7 (Bojana Ristic), 8-9 (Goran Djukanovic), 10–11 (Anibal Trejo), 12–13 (Erika Cross), 15 top right (Miguel Campos), 16–17 (Tsian), 18–19 (Dmitrydesign), 19 top right (TDC Photography), 20–21 (CyberEak), 24–25 (antb), 28 middle (Foto-Ruhrgebiet), 30–31 (Andreas Gradin), 31 middle right (jumpingsack), 34–35 (Christian Bertrand), 36–37 (Dusan Jankovic), 38 middle left (Peshkov Daniil), 38–39 (glen Gaffney), 40 middle left (Darko Zeljkovic), 40–41, 42–43 top (Christian Bertrand), 42–43.
NFL, Live Nation, Generation Records, Pepsi, Arm & Hammer and other manufacturers and brands are registered trademarks and/or are protected by copyright. They are usually given with a ™, ®, or © symbol.

Graphics: Stefan Chabluk

Library and Archives Canada Cataloguing in Publication

Perl, Sheri, author
        The economics of a rock concert / Sheri Perl.

(Economics of entertainment)
Includes index.
Issued in print and electronic formats.
ISBN 978-0-7787-7969-8 (bound).--ISBN 978-0-7787-7974-2 (pbk.).--ISBN 978-1-4271-7868-8 (pdf).--ISBN 978-1-4271-7983-8 (html)

        1. Rock music--Economic aspects--Juvenile literature. 2. Rock concerts--Production and direction--Juvenile literature. 3. Music trade--Juvenile literature. I. Title.

ML3790.P452 2014   j781.66   C2013-907575-5
                                                             C2013-907576-3

Library of Congress Cataloging-in-Publication Data

Perl, Sheri, 1967-, author.
  The economics of a rock concert / Sheri Perl.
      pages cm. -- (Economics of entertainment)
  Includes index.
  ISBN 978-0-7787-7969-8 (reinforced library binding) -- ISBN 978-0-7787-7974-2 (pbk.) -- ISBN 978-1-4271-7868-8 (electronic pdf) -- ISBN 978-1-4271-7983-8 (electronic html)
  1. Rock concerts--Economic aspects--Juvenile literature.
  2. Music trade--Juvenile literature. I. Title.

  ML3790.P43 2014
  781.66068--dc23

                              2013043400

Crabtree Publishing Company

Printed in Canada/022014/MA20131220

www.crabtreebooks.com   1-800-387-7650

Published in Canada
Crabtree Publishing
616 Welland Ave.
St. Catharines, ON
L2M 5V6

Published in the United States
Crabtree Publishing
PMB 59051
350 Fifth Avenue, 59th Floor
New York, New York 10118

Published in the United Kingdom
Crabtree Publishing
Maritime House
Basin Road North, Hove
BN41 1WR

Published in Australia
Crabtree Publishing
3 Charles Street
Coburg North
VIC, 3058

CONTENTS

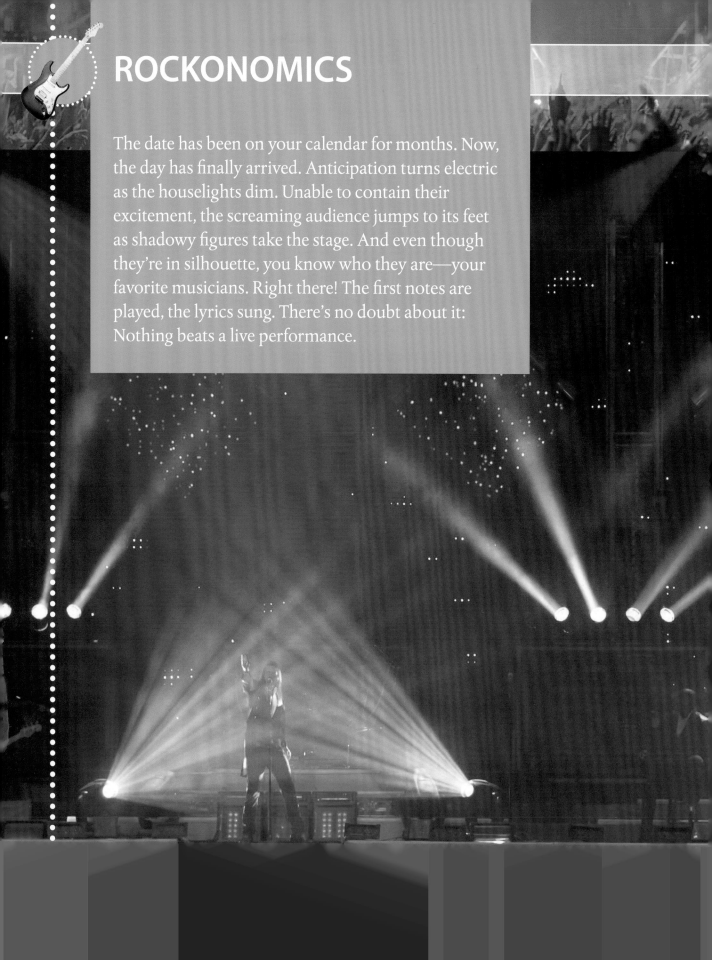

ROCKONOMICS

The date has been on your calendar for months. Now, the day has finally arrived. Anticipation turns electric as the houselights dim. Unable to contain their excitement, the screaming audience jumps to its feet as shadowy figures take the stage. And even though they're in silhouette, you know who they are—your favorite musicians. Right there! The first notes are played, the lyrics sung. There's no doubt about it: Nothing beats a live performance.

TICKETS, PLEASE!

Did you ever stop to wonder what made this concert possible? Who were the key players? What was needed to bring it from concept to concert? Who decided how much to charge for the tickets? Where does all the money from ticket sales and other **revenue streams** go? The discipline of **economics** can help you answer all of these questions. Economics deals with the **production** (putting on a concert), **distribution** (ticket sales), and consumption (by you) of goods and services (the concert).

WHAT DO YOU THINK?

First, consider your **cash flow** (money in and out) and monthly **fixed expenses** and **varied expenses**. With your **limited resources**, deciding between the things you need (food) and the things you want (a concert ticket) is sometimes tricky. Looking at the figures on the right, how many months will it take Liam to save for a ticket?

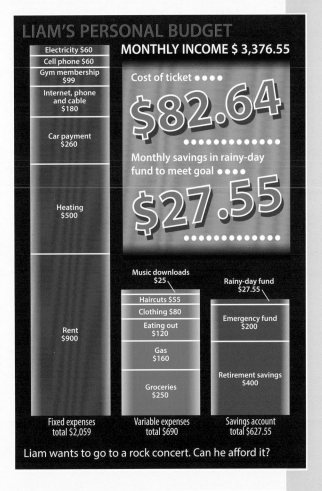

LIAM'S PERSONAL BUDGET

MONTHLY INCOME $ 3,376.55

Cost of ticket ● ● ● ●

$82.64

Monthly savings in rainy-day fund to meet goal ● ● ● ●

$27.55

Electricity $60
Cell phone $60
Gym membership $99
Internet, phone and cable $180
Car payment $260
Heating $500
Rent $900

Music downloads $25
Haircuts $55
Clothing $80
Eating out $120
Gas $160
Groceries $250

Rainy-day fund $27.55
Emergency fund $200
Retirement savings $400

Fixed expenses total $2,059 | Variable expenses total $690 | Savings account total $627.55

Liam wants to go to a rock concert. Can he afford it?

A MUSICAL IDEA!

FROM SMALL BEGINNINGS

It all starts with an idea. Someone at sometime said, "I bet I can make money by charging admission to hear musicians perform live." And they were correct! The concert industry has become a multi-billion dollar business. Today, this person in the concert industry is called the promoter. The promoter thinks of a band he or she wants to promote or present to the audience. Then he or she considers if the band can fill a stadium or a smaller venue (the facility where the concert will be held). Is it going to be a single-act show or a multi-act music festival?

IT HAD TO START SOMEWHERE

Many people believe the first live rock concert ever was the Moondog Coronation Ball in Cleveland, Ohio, on March 21, 1952. Alan Freed, or Moondog, a radio announcer, unknowingly became the first rock 'n' roll promoter, and as such is referred to as "the Father of Rock 'n' Roll." He knew how popular rhythm 'n' blues—the grandfather of rock 'n' roll—was among teenagers at the time. Freed thought he would sell tickets to an event featuring some of these artists for a live performance. Tickets were $1.50 in advance, or $1.75 at the door. Teens lined up eagerly and seats were sold out in minutes. Today, anyone looking in on this scene would view this as normal concert behavior. But at the time no one had ever even heard the phrase "rock concert." When about 25,000 fans showed up at the venue, which seated only 10,000, Freed knew he had stumbled upon a brand new market—the concert industry.

Due to supply and demand, tickets for a major rock concert—for maybe 20,000 seats—can sell out in less than 60 seconds. Amazing!

CONCERT TOURS

The 1960s marked the true beginning of concert tours. At first, however, most bands made their living predominately from record sales, not concerts. And, because of this, concert tickets were much cheaper than now. As the age of the Internet flourished and downloading music became wildly popular, the loss of profit for record sales reached an all-time low. The music industry had to revamp their ideas. Large-venue world tours became the new way artists made money. This change in the industry was brought on by you, the **consumer**. While the demand for records decreased and the demand for concert tickets increased, the cost for records dwindled while concert ticket prices sky-rocketed. This is called **supply and demand**.

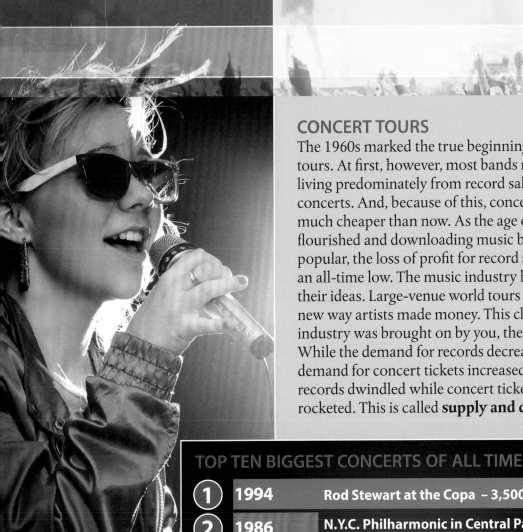

TOP TEN BIGGEST CONCERTS OF ALL TIME

1	1994	Rod Stewart at the Copa – 3,500,000
2	1986	N.Y.C. Philharmonic in Central Park – 800,000
3	1997	Garth Brooks in Central Park – 750,000
4	1983	Steve Wozniak's U.S. Festival – 670,000
5	1973	Summer Jam at Watkins Glen – 600,000 plus
6	1970	Isle of Wight Festival – 600,000
7	1981	Simon and Garfunkel Reunion – 500,000
8	2003	Toronto SARS Benefit – 450,000 plus
9	1969	Woodstock – 400,000
10	1997	Blockbuster RockFest – 385,000

Who has played to the most people in music history.

1 THE CONCERT INDUSTRY

Imagine you are a concert promoter. You love your job. It's fast-paced and ever-changing. You get to meet all types of exciting people, not only musicians, but all the people involved in putting on a concert. You and other key players in the music industry influence the global **economy**. But the greatest impact on a band's success is the consumer.

INSIDER INSIGHT

"As a rock star, I have two instincts ... to have fun and ... change the world. I have a chance to do both."
Bono of U2

At big rock concerts, tens of thousands of fans pay hundreds of dollars to hear and watch their favorite bands or singers.

A PIECE OF THE PIE

It takes hundreds of paid professionals to put on a rock concert. Some are paid a salary (weekly, monthly, or any regular income), while others are paid **commission** (a percentage from the **profit**). The profit is what's left over after you subtract the costs from the ticket sales and other revenue.

As the promoter, you earn perhaps 15 percent of the profit. But, before you make any money, you'll need to pay the venue upfront. Therefore, as a promoter, you begin at a loss of profit and hope you will not only **recoup** that money but make a profit. The venue will make 100 percent from all parking fees and, depending on the artist, 15 percent of all merchandise such as T-shirts and posters. What about the artist? Before they can make any money, they have a staff to pay!

WHAT DO YOU THINK?

Would you rather be paid a set salary, like the touring manager, or make a commission from the profits, like the artist's manager? Why?

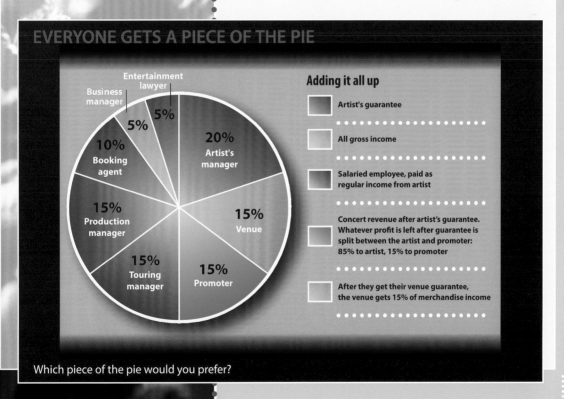

EVERYONE GETS A PIECE OF THE PIE

Pie chart segments:
- 20% Artist's manager
- 15% Venue
- 15% Promoter
- 15% Touring manager
- 15% Production manager
- 10% Booking agent
- 5% Business manager
- 5% Entertainment lawyer

Adding it all up

- **Artist's guarantee**
- **All gross income**
- **Salaried employee, paid as regular income from artist**
- **Concert revenue after artist's guarantee. Whatever profit is left after guarantee is split between the artist and promoter: 85% to artist, 15% to promoter**
- **After they get their venue guarantee, the venue gets 15% of merchandise income**

Which piece of the pie would you prefer?

FAN DEMAND

SUPPLY AND DEMAND

A concert is an **experience good**, a product you pay for before knowing its quality. The desire to hear musicians perform live is so strong that fans will pay almost anything. The concert industry is the only form of entertainment untouched by the recent economic **recession** (a period of high unemployment and failing businesses). Some goods will experience **deflation** (a decrease in the cost of goods) during a recession. However, concert tickets continue to experience **inflation** (the rising cost of goods). When a concert is sold out, there are not enough tickets to feed the demand of the fans. This is called **scarcity**. Devoted fans create such a fever that tickets become a hot commodity—a good with such appeal that the supply of the good cannot satisfy the demand, in turn driving the price of tickets up.

This is why concert tickets are so expensive. To purchase them, you will have to consider the **opportunity cost** and the **trade-off** you'll need to make. The trade-off is what you're willing to sacrifice in order to afford the tickets. Say you're willing to skip seeing seven movies to have the money to pay for your tickets. The trade-off is the movies for the concert tickets. The opportunity cost of the tickets is the dollar value of what you could have chosen to spend your money on instead of buying the tickets.

Our economic system is called the **free market**. The free market allows businesses, instead of the government, to set their own prices. Free markets allow people to make choices about their own spending.

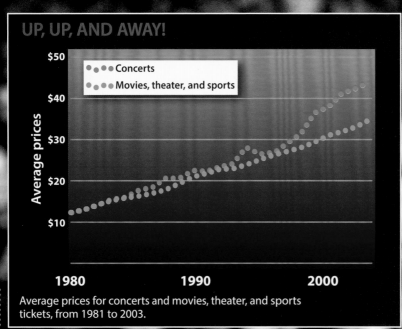

UP, UP, AND AWAY!

- Concerts
- Movies, theater, and sports

Average prices for concerts and movies, theater, and sports tickets, from 1981 to 2003.

Samuel Titos, member of Dover, performs to large crowds in Barcelona, Spain, on September 22, 2012.

WHAT DO YOU THINK?

Put these examples of goods in order, from most likely to least likely to meet the demand of consumers: an Apple iPad, tickets to see an NFL game, clothing, tickets to see Justin Timberlake, food, and tickets to a Broadway show. Besides the Justin Timberlake tickets, which of these is most like the concert industry?

2 FROM CONCEPT TO CONCERT

No matter the size of the fan base or the popularity of an artist, all concerts begin with the same three components: talent, venue, and **marketing**. To choose the appropriately sized venue, a promoter must consider the talent, or artist, and his or her popularity. If you predict the artist can sell out the venue, then you have a match and can move forward with an offer to the talent's agent. Only then will you begin the last step, which is marketing or advertising the concert.

Madison Square Garden is home to the NY Knicks, NY Rangers, and NY Liberty, but it is also one of the largest indoor concert arenas in the world.

THE RECORD BREAKERS

Live Nation Entertainment is the largest producer and promoter of live music events in the world (according to Live Nation). Live Nation owns and operates 84 venues. If you've seen a concert, chances are you saw it in a venue owned by Live Nation.

IT'S AS EASY AS ONE, TWO, THREE: STEP ONE—THE TALENT

First up is to identify the talent you want to promote. If it's BIG talent, such as One Direction or Bruno Mars, then you will likely be able to fill a large stadium and your show will sell out in record time. However, lesser-known artists, such as Alt-J or Vampire Weekend, may not have the same draw . . . yet! After all, not everyone can sell out Madison Square Garden. The name of the game is to make a profit. For that reason, a promoter must always think in terms of how many seats will sell.

Say you book a large venue of 20,000 seats with an unknown artist. Most likely, he or she will be unable to fill those seats and you will take a hit or suffer a loss of profit. A loss of profit is when the cost is more than the revenue (the money made before costs are subtracted) and you are in the **negative numbers**! That's very bad.

Think: Big names = big venues; lesser known artists = smaller concert halls. Here's another way to think about it: The more seats sold, the more revenue generated, therefore, the more profit earned. For that reason, fitting the right artist to the correct-sized venue is vital, not only to your success as a promoter but to your hard-earned reputation of knowing your industry well and your ability to correctly judge a talent's appeal!

STEP TWO—THE VENUE

The next step is to put the venue on hold. Then, contact the talent's agent, tell them your vision, that you have the venue on hold, and make your offer. If the artist is going on a world tour, many promoters from all over the world will also be contacting the agent. Likewise, the artist will have several agents specializing in specific territories. Some artists have touring managers who keep the world tour well organized. All of these people—the various promoters, touring managers, and agents—work together to create the itinerary for the tour. Once all of them agree to the terms, each promoter will pay rent to their selected venue. The promoter then prepares a **budget**, projecting costs, sales, and profits. The promoter will also hire people to perfect sound, lighting, and other technical aspects. Catering and security crews are also hired. When the artist agrees to the terms, you can then move on to the final step.

STEP THREE—MARKETING

Marketing, or promoting, the concert is the final step. The goal of promotion is to excite fans about the concert tour. There are many ways this can be done, such as through print ads, newspapers, flyers, and billboards. Radio announcements account for a large percentage of concert promotion. But the most effective marketing tool today is social media such as Facebook, Twitter, and Instagram. Most artists have their own Twitter accounts. Talent … check! Venue … check! Marketing … check!

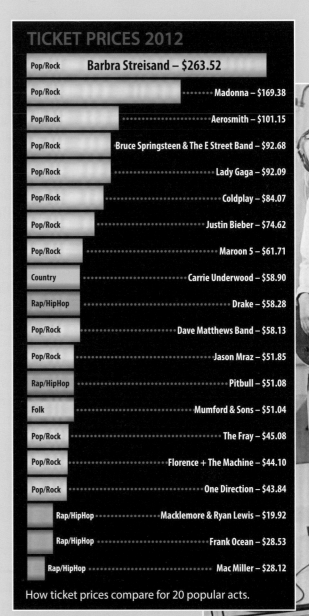

TICKET PRICES 2012

Pop/Rock	Barbra Streisand – $263.52
Pop/Rock	Madonna – $169.38
Pop/Rock	Aerosmith – $101.15
Pop/Rock	Bruce Springsteen & The E Street Band – $92.68
Pop/Rock	Lady Gaga – $92.09
Pop/Rock	Coldplay – $84.07
Pop/Rock	Justin Bieber – $74.62
Pop/Rock	Maroon 5 – $61.71
Country	Carrie Underwood – $58.90
Rap/HipHop	Drake – $58.28
Pop/Rock	Dave Matthews Band – $58.13
Pop/Rock	Jason Mraz – $51.85
Rap/HipHop	Pitbull – $51.08
Folk	Mumford & Sons – $51.04
Pop/Rock	The Fray – $45.08
Pop/Rock	Florence + The Machine – $44.10
Pop/Rock	One Direction – $43.84
Rap/HipHop	Macklemore & Ryan Lewis – $19.92
Rap/HipHop	Frank Ocean – $28.53
Rap/HipHop	Mac Miller – $28.12

How ticket prices compare for 20 popular acts.

There are many people who work behind the scenes to get music out into the world. Here, a music producer adjusts the sound mixer during a recording session.

THE RECORD BREAKERS

- Over 30 percent of teens in the U.S.A. attended a concert in 2012
- 85 percent of adults listen to music an average of 3.5 hours every day
- 58 percent of Americans say music is an integral part of their lives
- 60 percent of concert goers are likely to purchase a product from a sponsor

It's all part of the big picture! Signing autographs for eager fans, singer Enrique Bunbury promotes his new album in Mexico City, Mexico, in 2010.

TO MARKET, TO MARKET

RIHANNA'S ALBUM *LOUD*
Rihanna's album *LOUD* released in 2010, cost her record label $1,078,000 in its two-week writing camp. At the end of the two weeks, all the songs for *LOUD* had been written and approved by Rihanna.

Radio promotion of concerts is one of the easiest ways to advertise a concert.

MARKETING

Marketing is more than just radio announcements and tweets. Television interviews are another way to promote music. Fans love to see the personalities of their favorite artists. They love to know the story behind the public persona they portray. Another marketing tool is autographs. Often, music stores, such as Generation Records in New York City, will hold artist signings, where fans line up with something for an artist to sign such as a poster or T-shirt. It's that chance to get close to a star.

WRITING CAMP

Musicians, such as the Eagles or Paul McCartney, have proven track records of producing hit after hit. Their name alone is enough to draw sold-out audiences to their concerts without needing to produce any new music. But for today's newer musicians, such as Rihanna, it is necessary for them to first produce a new album with at least one hit song. These artists need a hit song that saturates the radio. A musician's record label, manager, and agent sometimes spend close to $1 million to create a hit song. One way to do this is through a writing camp. Writing camp is an opportunity for an artist's team to hire the best songwriters and musicians from all over the world to come together for two solid weeks of songwriting. At the end of those two weeks, the artist will approve every song that will appear on their next album. Anticipation rises as the waiting game begins. Will any of the songs be a hit? If so, the **investment** was worthwhile.

WHAT DO YOU THINK?

Economists say you have to spend money to make money. This seems to be what the music industry believes. Can you think of a time in your life when you may be willing to take such a risk?

IT'S SHOWTIME!

ON THE ROAD

Before you know it, it's time to take the whole show on the road. This is the moment when your concept turns into an actual concert. Remember that production is the making of goods and services. Production is involved in creating an album and making merchandise to sell. But the biggest part of producing a rock concert is the concert itself!

One of the most complex tasks in producing a concert is building the stage. Modern stages can be quite elaborate, with multi-levels and cranes that lift singers up and over the audience while rotating nearly 360 degrees. Many shows feature huge LED (light-emitting diode) screens, pyrotechnics, fog machines, lasers, and confetti airbursts that rain down confetti from up above the audience. All of these special effects create jobs for roadies, or skilled laborers.

For large acts such as Aerosmith it can take as many as 200 roadies to produce a concert. About 20 semi-trucks will arrive on the scene with the band's equipment and begin unloading and setting everything up. About 100 miles (161 km) of electric cable will need to be unraveled and more than 600 lights will need to be hung. It takes as much electricity to put on a rock concert as to power a 25-story building! It begins at 8 A.M. and, in as little as 12 hours, the arena is ready to go. At the end of the night, the roadies will tear it all down. What took 12 hours to set up takes about 2.5 hours to pack away. Then it's on to the next city!

Because of the **human resources** (skilled laborers) needed to produce a concert, concerts feed the job market and fuel the economy. So, the next time you buy a concert ticket, you can feel good knowing that you've just created jobs for many people.

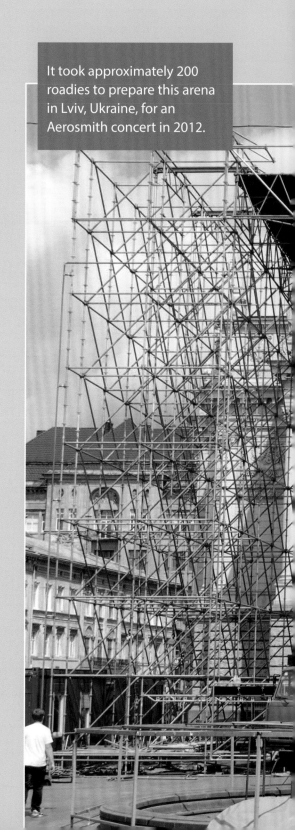

It took approximately 200 roadies to prepare this arena in Lviv, Ukraine, for an Aerosmith concert in 2012.

TRICKS OF THE TRADE

Can you be overprepared? Aerosmith's lead guitarist Joe Perry tours with 42 guitars! He wants to be ready for any possibility that may come his way. Twenty-one of these are his main guitars, while the other 21 are backups. Of all his guitars, Billie is his favorite, named after his wife Billie Montgomery.

Joe Perry, lead guitarist for Aerosmith, playing at the Pepsi Center in Denver, Colorado.

3 WHO'S RESPONSIBLE?

Before a profit can be made, a few items need to be settled or reconciled. There are many upfront costs in concert promotion such as the rent for the venue. Some costs need to be paid at the end of the night such as the caterer, road crew, and even state taxes. All of these costs need to be resolved between the promoter and the artist. Who pays for what?

Linkin Park performs live during their A Thousand Suns World Tour on September 23, 2011, in Bangkok, Thailand.

PROMOTER'S RESPONSIBILITY

The rent for the venue is one of the largest upfront costs a promoter has. Most large arenas cost an average of $80,000 for one night. Therefore, most concert promotions begin "in the red," which is a phrase used to express a profit loss or debt. The goal is to get your numbers "in the black" at the end of the concert. "In the black" means earning a profit or being **financially solvent**. "In the red" and "in the black" are phrases that go back to when accounting was done in a book with pen and paper. Red ink was used to show money owed, while black ink was used to show profit.

The promoter's production team and the artist's production team discuss all the requirements necessary, from labor to any types of audio, sound, and lighting. However, most artists these days travel with their own equipment. All expenses to do with dressing rooms and special requests, such as catering, are also discussed and agreed upon upfront. All of these expenses are put into what's called a rider, an upfront agreement managing the expectations of each leg of the world tour. Most of these items are, at first, paid for by the promoter but then settled, or paid back to the promoter, at the end of the night.

Then, when the box office totals the revenue from the concert, all the expenses are subtracted and paid to the promoter, venue, crews, and venue staff. After that, a profit split will be shared between the artist and the promoter. You will learn more about profit splitting later.

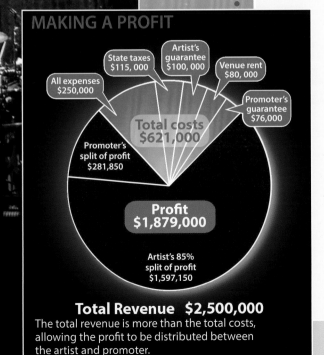

MAKING A PROFIT

All expenses $250,000
State taxes $115,000
Artist's guarantee $100,000
Venue rent $80,000
Promoter's guarantee $76,000

Total costs $621,000

Promoter's split of profit $281,850

Profit $1,879,000

Artist's 85% split of profit $1,597,150

Total Revenue $2,500,000
The total revenue is more than the total costs, allowing the profit to be distributed between the artist and promoter.

TAKING A PROFIT

THERE ARE NO GUARANTEES

You've probably heard the quote, "There are no guarantees," but in the music business there are two—the artist's **guarantee** and the promoter's guarantee. Remember, in the planning stages of the concert, the popularity of the artist was considered in order to choose the right venue. Another cost needed to be considered then, too. The artist's guarantee is the amount of money the artist is paid for the concert regardless of revenue generated or profit earned. The guarantee is **non-negotiable** for big names. Say you want to book Beyoncé. Before you can **project** your budget, you need to know her guarantee. The promoter also has a guarantee, usually less than the artist's. Once all costs are subtracted from the concert's revenue, the remaining profit is split—85 percent to the artist and 15 percent to the promoter. This is called profit splitting or profit sharing.

INSIDER INSIGHT

"I grew up listening to Jay-Z, and I think the first time I really became obsessed with learning and thinking about lyrics was when I started listening to rap."
Ezra Koenig, lead singer and guitarist of Vampire Weekend

Glastonbury Festival contributes more than £100 ($163) million annually to the British economy.

BACKING INTO THE BUDGET

Concert economics is a backward math puzzle. You start with the venue rent and guarantees, then work in your numbers. The venue holds 10,000 seats and the average cost of a ticket is $50. What is the **gross** profit before costs are subtracted?

Other costs:

Rent: $50,000
Artist's guarantee: $50,000
Promoter's guarantee: $40,000
Marketing: $75,000
Labor: $25,000
Production costs: $25,000

Subtracting these from the gross profit, what would it **yield** in pure profit?

TOP 20 TOURING ARTISTS

MILLIONS of DOLLARS

Rank	Artist	Live Concerts	Recordings	Publishing	Total Income
1	Paul McCartney	64.9	2.2	2.2	72.1
2	The Rolling Stones	39.6	0.9	2.2	44.0
3	Dave Matthews Band	27.9	0.0	2.5	31.3
4	Celine Dion	22.4	3.1	0.9	31.1
5	Eminem	5.5	10.4	3.8	28.9
6	Cher	26.2	0.5	0.0	26.7
7	Bruce Springsteen	17.9	2.2	4.5	24.8
8	Jay-Z	0.7	12.7	0.7	22.7
9	Ozzy Osbourne/the Osbournes	3.8	0.2	0.5	22.5
10	Elton John	20.2	0.9	1.3	22.4
11	The Eagles	15.1	0.7	1.4	17.6
12	Jimmy Buffett	13.7	0.2	0.5	17.6
13	Billy Joel	16.0	0.0	1.0	17.0
14	Neil Diamond	16.5	0.0	0.3	16.8
15	Aerosmith	11.6	1.0	0.8	16.5
16	Crosby, Stills, Nash & Young	15.7	0.0	0.3	16.0
17	Creed	10.9	1.1	1.6	13.4
18	Rush	13.4	0.0	0.0	13.4
19	Linkin Park	1.7	4.7	6.3	13.1
20	The Who	12.6	0.0	0.0	12.6

The total pre-tax gross income earned by 20 selected touring artists. (rounded figures)

4 TICKETS AND PRICING

Once the stage layout is determined, the promoter, artist's manager, and venue owners walk the arena, deciding which seats cannot be sold due to obstructed views and which seats will be sold as **VIP** seating (the highest priced, closest-to-the-stage seats). From this, a seating manifest, or plan, is created and tickets go on sale. But how do they decide how much to charge? And why do tickets sell out so quickly?

Fans wait to hear American pop diva Lady Gaga in Singapore in 2012. Faced with the recession back home, more Western musicians are lured to Asia where **disposable income** is common.

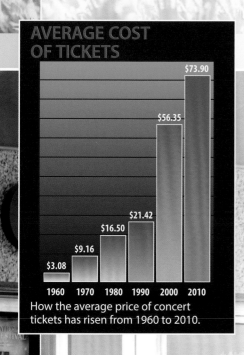

AVERAGE COST OF TICKETS

1960	$3.08
1970	$9.16
1980	$16.50
1990	$21.42
2000	$56.35
2010	$73.90

How the average price of concert tickets has risen from 1960 to 2010.

INSIDER INSIGHT

In 1980, you could buy a ticket to see Bruce Springsteen for $9.50. In 2012, the average ticket price for a Bruce concert was $92.68, plus fees.

"Over the past four decades, two hours of live music moved from the entertainment column of the family budget to the category of major purchase."
Rick Chase, journalist

CHA-CHING!

Here's how promoters calculate what to charge for tickets: They consider the cost of the venue, the artist's guarantee, projected costs, and the projected revenue. Then they price the tickets accordingly to offset those overall costs. Supply and demand of the tickets come into play, too. If it's a high-profile artist who rarely tours, then those tickets will be in high demand, allowing them to charge BIG ticket prices.

Since you can't guarantee a sell-out, VIP packages are created to secure additional money. These packages offer the best seats in the house, an artist meet-and-greet, a photo opportunity with the artist, an autograph, and usually merchandise. Depending on the artist, VIP seats can cost anywhere from $500 for Maroon 5 to $2,000 for Justin Timberlake. Other more important artists who rarely tour, such as former Beatle Paul McCartney, could sell VIP passes for as much as $5,000.

SOLD OUT ALREADY?

Tickets are not only sold to fans. They are also sold to radio stations, credit card companies, and other corporations. These tickets are then given away in promotions, to the artist's fan club to win in contests, and to the band's family and friends. As a result, a number of tickets are unavailable for sale to the general public.

So, the next time you hear that a venue has 15,000 seats, you'll know that fewer tickets are available for sale to consumers like you. In fact, between the band's family and friends and give-aways, maybe only 2,000 out of the 15,000 seats are left for purchase. The hotter the show and the bigger and more popular the artist, the less likely you are to grab any tickets for the concert.

PRICE DISCRIMINATION

Backstage passes give fans a rare opportunity to see behind the scenes of a concert and perhaps meet the artist.

Natalie Grant performs in GMC's Uplift Someone America Bus Tour at Stone Mountain Park in Georgia in 2011.

FOR THE PROMOTER

In the music business, **price discrimination** is a way of offering a variety of **price points** to fans with different **incomes**. One reason for staggering prices is to protect the promoter's investment in the cost of the venue.

Obviously, the promoter's goal is to earn a profit. While it's true that higher-priced seats yield greater revenue, a promoter could not sell out a concert if all 15,000 seats were set at the highest VIP price. If you charged everyone $2,000 a seat, your focus would be narrow, only attracting those with the most disposable income (money left over after necessities, such as rent, food, and clothing, have been paid). Think of it like a beam of light in the dark when you want to see as much as possible.

THE RECORD BREAKERS

According to research by editor Marlow Stern, Vampire Weekend was the most traveled band in 2010, covering approx. 150,000 miles (241,400 km). That's a little more than half the distance to travel from Earth to the Moon!

STADIUM SEATING PRICES

Section	Lowest	Highest
PINK UPPER LEVEL SEATING (NOSE BLEED)	$73	$806
BLUE MAIN LEVEL SEATING	$115	$884
PURPLE MEZZANINE SEATING	$120	$862
RED HALL OF FAME SEATING	$144	$880
GREEN FIELD SEATING	$167	$1,139
YELLOW PIT SEATING	$3,400	$3,400
TURQUOISE SUITE SEATS	$9,400	$14,900

The price of tickets for the Taylor Swift concert held on May 25, 2013, at the Cowboys Stadium in Texas.

If your beam of light is narrow, you can only see a sliver. But if you open your lens so that the beam is wide, you can see much more. For promoters, price discrimination is widening the beam of light that is cast on the fan base.

FOR THE FANS

Since you and your friends do not have the same **earning capacity** (or pocket money), you cannot all afford the same things. As you now know, the concert is the product in our example and is an experience good.

But is this product the same for everyone? Chances are it isn't. Those in the first row may be lucky enough to reach up and touch the lead singer. Should a fan in the back row pay the same price? Discrimination offers a balance in the price inequity of the venue's seating.

WHAT DO YOU THINK?

How would the price of tickets be affected if fewer were given away to the band's family and friends or as giveaways? How does price discrimination help you as a consumer? How does it hurt you?

BRANDING A BAND

CREATING A BRAND

One way to ensure the success of an artist is to create a **brand**. Branding attracts a target audience (a specific group of people). It includes everything from the types of music the artists perform to the clothes they wear, the haircut they rock, and whether they use heavy black eyeliner and black nail polish or have a more clean-cut image.

Managers and agents work very hard creating an image for the musician to target a specific gender, age, and/or **income bracket**. Everything is carefully calculated with this target audience in mind.

Compare, for example, the fans of Justin Bieber to the fans of Muse. Are they the same target audience? Justin Bieber's fans tend to be girls between the ages of 10 and 15. Muse tends to have more male fans than female, ranging in age between 15 and 30.

BRAND EXTENSIONS

Once an artist has been branded, it's time to create other revenue streams (a way to make money). One way is through brand extensions, which is taking a product known for a specific feature and creating a spinoff product that is closely related to the original to create more sales to the same target audience. For example, in the food industry, one such brand extension is Arm & Hammer baking soda toothpaste from Arm & Hammer baking soda.

In terms of a musician's brand extensions while on tour, this would be concert T-shirts, posters, concert programs, and accessories with the band's logo on them. But brand extensions can continue outside the realm of touring. Many musicians have their own perfume and/or beverage lines. These are brand extensions.

WHAT DO YOU THINK?

Let's get creative! Create a band. Give it a name and a brand image. Describe your target audience and think of some possible brand extensions.

THE RECORD BREAKERS

In 2010, about 80,000 people attended the Bonnaroo Festival in Manchester, Tennessee, and produced about 489 tons (444 metric tons) of waste and 130 tons (118 metric tons) of recycled waste. The average total amount spent by each attendee for the four days was $1,440. This expense included the cost of tickets, travel, hotel, food, drinks, and souvenirs.

The heavy metal band Death Maze performs live at the outdoor festival, Kulturnatta in Umeå, Sweden, on May 21, 2011.

Sales from merchandise, such as T-shirts and posters, offer additional revenue streams for artists.

A WORD FROM OUR SPONSOR

AFTER-PARTY SPONSORS

After a large concert, there is often a party referred to as an after-party. After-parties can be lavish and expensive, and are usually for the band and their entourage. Most of these after-parties are sponsored, meaning they are paid for by large companies. Sometimes, there are many **sponsors**, each paying for something specific. Sometimes there is only one sponsor, fronting the whole event. Some parties have been known to feature a bar made completely of carved ice, sponsored by a well-known drink company. Why would a company do such a thing for an artist?

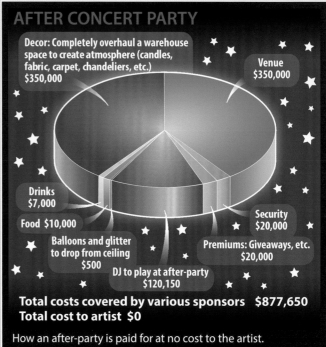

AFTER CONCERT PARTY

Decor: Completely overhaul a warehouse space to create atmosphere (candles, fabric, carpet, chandeliers, etc.) $350,000

Venue $350,000

Drinks $7,000

Food $10,000

Balloons and glitter to drop from ceiling $500

DJ to play at after-party $120,150

Premiums: Giveaways, etc. $20,000

Security $20,000

Total costs covered by various sponsors $877,650
Total cost to artist $0

How an after-party is paid for at no cost to the artist.

ENDORSEMENTS

An endorsement is another type of sponsorship an artist can have. This type of sponsorship is not about lavish after-parties. With an endorsement, a company offers the musician a contract to be their spokesperson. This means the artist will appear in print and TV ads using their product. Often, musicians will sing the theme song for the product.

Successful endorsements relate to branding. If your musician is branded as an honest, sweet, clean-cut teen, then some possible sponsors to compliment his image may be soda companies. Sponsors mean big money for musicians. However, the musicians can't do anything to tarnish their image. Once they do, the endorsement ends. Sponsors are eager to throw money at big-name musicians in the hope that they will endorse their product. They want the public to see the band drinking their soda, driving their car, or wearing their sneakers. And if photographers capture a picture of a musician with their product, even better!

The audience enjoys Queen during a charity anti-AIDS concert on June 30, 2012, in Kyev, Ukraine.

THE BUDGET

Creating a careful budget is vital to your reputation as a promoter. You must consider every possible cost. Most crews are **union** employees. Union salaries and the cost of the venue are readily available information, so not much guesswork is needed. Experience and knowledge are a promoter's best friends. You are only as good as the accuracy of your estimated budget. That is basic economics.

COLLEGE BAND BUDGET

COSTS

Signs $4
Stage $120
Barricade $85
Damaged microphone $86
Tickets $118
Flyers $136
Food for artists $150
Damaged barrier $155
Trade-show booth $180
Event lead staff $189
Sound $200
Lights $200
Parking permits $258
Police $455
Clear room $504
Staff $716
Insurance $1,792.42
Artists $5,950

Profit $1,167.08

Total $11,298.42

TICKET PRICES SALES

At Door - 157 at $10 $1,570
Online - 205 at $7 $1,435
Presale - 350 at $5 $1,750
Fundraising $268.50
Dean's Fund $400
Sponsorship $750
Insurance $1,660

Total $12,465.50

FUNDING REVISED BUDGET

STUDENT PROGRAMMING FUNDING BOARD $4,632

The budget for a small-venue concert at a college.

STAYING ON BUDGET

Someone on the promoter's team is responsible for making sure everything stays on budget. This person is the production manager. Production managers have a schedule of the day for all the crews. It is their job to make sure everyone stays right on schedule. A good production manager will always add into their budget overtime for union workers.

A typical day setting up for a concert could run like this:
8:00 A.M.–12:00 P.M.: Set-up, sound check, lighting, and special effects
12:00–1:00 P.M.: Lunchtime
1:00–6:00 P.M.: More setting-up, sound, lighting, special effects
6:00–8:00 P.M.: Dinner break
8:00–11:00 P.M.: Showtime!
If the show runs past 11:00 P.M., overtime fees start adding up. It's all about effective time management.

SMALL-VENUE BUDGET

Remember price discrimination? A small venue cannot offer much variety in the way of seating prices because of its size. Most seats offer similar views and experiences. While a fan can expect some price discrimination, you see a much broader range with larger arenas. The challenge of a small venue for a promoter is having to ensure that most seats sell, because you won't have big-ticket VIP seats to offset losses on unsold seats. The advantage of a small venue is that it gives lesser-known bands the opportunity to increase their audience and test their market.

The Rapture performs at Razzmatazz in Barcelona, Spain, on November 22, 2011.

LARGE-VENUE BUDGET

LARGE-VENUE PROBLEMS

While large stadiums offer more opportunities for fans to grab tickets, they possess many potential problems for a promoter. First, big events are much more expensive to produce. Therefore, the financial risk a promoter takes by laying out the money upfront is far greater. Second, the sheer number of human resources needed to set up the concert is an immense operation. Usually, big venues mean very complicated stages. The bigger the operation, the more people involved, and the more likely problems will arise. It takes a team of people on the promoter's side, the artist's side, and the venue's side to make sure everything goes off without a hitch.

TRICKS OF THE TRADE

On December 19, 2010, Muse performed at the Steel Blue Oval in Western Australia. With only one exit, it took hours for tens of thousands of fans to leave the outdoor arena.

THE VENUE'S PROFITS

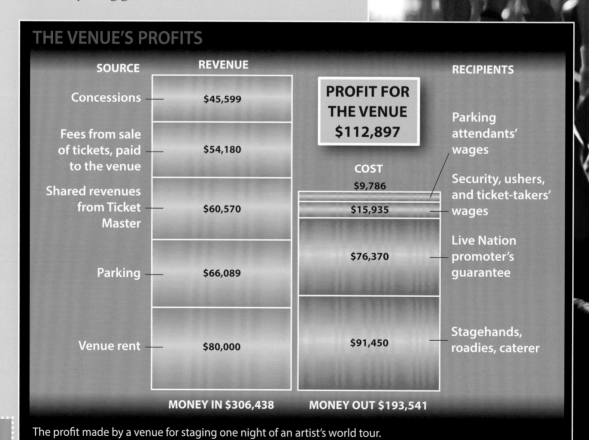

SOURCE	REVENUE		RECIPIENTS
Concessions	$45,599	**PROFIT FOR THE VENUE $112,897**	
Fees from sale of tickets, paid to the venue	$54,180		Parking attendants' wages
		COST	Security, ushers, and ticket-takers' wages
Shared revenues from Ticket Master	$60,570	$9,786	
		$15,935	
Parking	$66,089	$76,370	Live Nation promoter's guarantee
Venue rent	$80,000	$91,450	Stagehands, roadies, caterer
MONEY IN $306,438		**MONEY OUT $193,541**	

The profit made by a venue for staging one night of an artist's world tour.

Crowd control is a serious issue at any concert—indoor, outdoor, large, or small.

THE RECORD BREAKERS

Following 2009's No Line On The Horizon Tour, U2 embarked on their massive 360° Tour. The tour was a two-year global romp that brought in about $736 million in revenue—and nearly $200 million more than The Rolling Stones' A Bigger Bang Tour.

THE THINGS UNSEEN

Bad weather can have huge effects on a concert budget. Heavy rain or snow can close a venue or prevent people from getting there on time.

WEATHER PERMITTING

Even though a concert budget is pretty much a science, there is always the potential for unforeseen things to suddenly throw your budget off track. The biggest things to affect your budget are delays in setting-up, things that stop set-up, or shows running past 11 P.M. By far the biggest culprit of such delays is Mother Nature, of course!

Remember, most tours travel from country to country, state to state, and city to city. Plane or truck delays due to bad weather can mean you have crews sitting at the venue with no semi-trucks to unload. The clock is ticking, workers will be paid, but no work is getting done. There is nothing you can do but wait. Waiting can be frustrating as you watch your budget slip away.

OTHER SETBACKS

Since most bands travel by bus, it is often very easy for someone to get sick. Due to the close-quarters of a tour bus, illnesses can spread rapidly from band member to band member. Most performers will push through illnesses that would put the rest of us straight to bed—but the show must go on. Canceling shows due to a performer's illness can have a serious impact on your budget. So when a show is canceled, it usually happens for a very good reason.

Rarely, injuries can occur for crew members or fans. If the crowd control is not well-maintained, resulting injuries can lead to lawsuits. Such lawsuits can be an enormous drain on a budget. Many promoters, agents, and artists take out **insurance** to cover the cost of any problems.

TEN HIGHEST-GROSSING TOURS OF 2012

	Total Gross ($ millions)	Total attendance	Number of shows
1 MADONNA	228.4	1,635,176	72
2 BRUCE SPRINGSTEEN & THE E STREET BAND	199.4	2,165,925	72
3 ROGER WATERS	186.5	1,680,042	72
4 MICHAEL JACKSON THE IMMORTAL WORLD TOUR (by Cirque Du Soleil)	147.3	1,374,482	183
5 COLDPLAY	147.3	1,811,787	67
6 LADY GAGA	124.9	1,111,099	65
7 KENNY CHESNEY & TIM McGRAW	96.5	1,085,382	23
8 VAN HALEN	54.4	522,296	46
9 JAY-Z & KANYE WEST	47	371,777	31
10 ANDRÉ RIEU	46.8	490,165	99

Who grossed what in 2012, and how many people saw them.

WHAT DO YOU THINK?

According to the table above, the top three highest-grossing tours of 2012 were musicians who have a wide appeal with an adult target audience. Using what you now know about economics, what do you think is the reason these mostly adult crowds resulted in the highest-grossing tours?

6 ROCKING ON

Promoters don't only look for huge sell-out tours. They also keep their ear to the ground hoping to discover the next new talent. There is no such thing as an overnight success. Musicians spend years and years—maybe even most of their lives—sharpening their acts. And then, something happens. Some connection clicks into place. After all that hard work, a tipping point occurs to take them to that next level. What—or who—tips the scales in their favor?

According to an American survey conducted in 2012, nearly 49.2 percent of teens spend $0 a month on music, because they download it for free; 54 percent have a music app on their smartphone; and 64 percent listen to music through YouTube. Some teens do all three.

YOU ARE IN CONTROL

Teens create today's music trends. Consumers have the power to determine what products or goods will be produced. This is called consumer sovereignty. In terms of the music business, consumer sovereignty occurs by simply clicking "like" on social media sites such as YouTube. Consumers decide which videos go viral. Before a musician can even grab a pen to sign on with an agent, she (or he) can go from singing alone in her bedroom to 5,000,000 hits in a few days. Today, it takes one hit song to propel the artist to that next level. Social networking sites put the consumer directly in the driver's seat of the music business. With the click of the thumbs-up button, they cast a vote sealing the fate of a song and its artist.

WARP SPEED AHEAD

Justin Bieber, Cody Simpson, Soulja Boy, Walk Off The Earth, and Colbie Caillat—what do these people have in common? They were all discovered on the Internet. There is no doubt about it: The Internet sets a career path for warp speed. In the 1960s, bands grew their reputations slowly, one record at a time. Fans had a long-term relationship with their favorite musicians. However, with the quick road to success for some of today's musicians, they can find themselves unprepared to deal with their "overnight success." Therefore, having a strong team of managers, agents, and promoters can be vital to the longevity of their career.

THE HIGHEST-GROSSING U.S. TOURS IN 2011

1. U2: $293,281,487; 44 shows
2. Bon Jovi: $192,947,951; 68 shows
3. Take That: $185,175,360; 29 shows
4. Roger Waters: $149,904,965; 92 shows
5. Taylor Swift: $97,368,416; 89 shows
6. Kenny Chesney: $84,576,917; 55 shows
7. Usher: $74,954,681; 73 shows
8. Lady Gaga: $71,900,434; 45 shows
9. André Rieu: $67,104,756; 102 shows
10. Sade $53,178,550; 59 shows

LOOKING TO THE FUTURE

INDUSTRY PREDICTIONS

Artist manager Jeff Rabhan, in his article "Music Industry Predictions: Labels, Concerts, Licensing and More," predicted a future for music that is already coming true. He believes the hard-ticket stub is on its way out the door to join up with vinyl records and the Sony Walkman. Most people purchase, or buy, tickets online. Rabhan believes that soon concert-goers will simply swipe their smartphones for entrance into a concert. Some experts predict smaller, more personal venues will become the next thing. At higher prices, they can offer fans a more intimate experience listening to their favorite bands perform live.

STREAMING VERSUS LIVE

Although nothing beats the live experience, sometimes a concert is too far away or expensive, making a fan's ability to see it live impossible. What's the next best thing to experiencing a concert live? Seeing it

INSIDER INSIGHT

"Ever since I was younger, I wanted to be on stage, singing my songs in a glittering costume. And that happened and is still happening. I have to remember that this is what I wished for and be grateful."
Katy Perry, singer

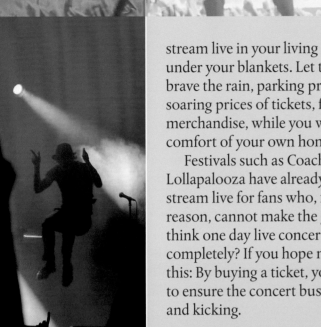

stream live in your living room, snuggled under your blankets. Let the other fans brave the rain, parking problems, and the soaring prices of tickets, food, drinks, and merchandise, while you watch from the comfort of your own home.

Festivals such as Coachella and Lollapalooza have already begun to stream live for fans who, for whatever reason, cannot make the gig. Do you think one day live concerts will disappear completely? If you hope not, remember this: By buying a ticket, you cast your vote to ensure the concert business stays alive and kicking.

WHAT DO YOU THINK?

Turn back to the figures on page 41. For each artist, divide the gross earnings by the number of shows performed to calculate the average gross earned for each show. Now reorder the artists. Are they in different order? How does taking the number of shows into consideration affect the order?

THE RECORD BREAKERS

According to Live Nation, in 2009, live music was the second-most-popular form of entertainment: about 52.1 million people attended concerts that year, while 73.4 million people attended baseball games.

The future of the music business lies in YOUR hands!

GLOSSARY

brand A name, symbol, or design that differentiates a product from other products

budget A financial plan that considers one's total income and expenses

cash flow A way to measure money coming in and going out

commission A varied income based on earning a percentage from the revenue generated, usually relating to sales

consumer A person who buys goods and services

deflation A decrease in the cost of goods

disposable income The amount of money left over after all living expenses have been paid

distribution Supplying products to businesses that sell them to consumers

earning capacity The amount of money one can potentially earn

economics The study of the manufacture, distribution, sale, and use of goods and services

economy The way a country manages its money and other resources to produce, buy, and sell its goods and services

entrepreneur Someone who comes up with an idea to create a business

experience good A product you pay for before knowing its quality

financially solvent Being able to meet financial obligations and pay debts

fixed expenses The expenses in your budget that do not change

free market An economy based on supply and demand with little or no government control

gross A company's revenue minus the cost of goods sold

guarantee The amount of money in a contract paid regardless of profit or loss

human resources People and the skills they possess to perform a task

incomes How much money people earn for the work they do or things they sell

income bracket People who have a similar income

inflation A rise in the cost of goods

insurance Financial protection against loss or other mishaps

investment The money an investor or promoter puts into a business

GLOSSARY

limited resources The finite amount of money each of us has

marketing The advertising, delivery, and selling of a service or good by targeting a specific audience

negative numbers Figures that occur when a company owes more money than it makes in profit

non-negotiable Not up for discussion

opportunity cost Things you give up when making a choice

price discrimination A marketing strategy in which a company charges customers different prices for the same product

price point A range in price an individual can afford based on their limited resources and income

production Making and providing goods and services for people to buy

profit The amount of money that a company makes after all the costs of running the business have been paid

project To forward-plan a budget by predicting costs and revenue

recession A period of high unemployment and failing businesses; the opposite of "growth"

recoup To regain, through profits, money that was spent or lost

revenue stream A niche or gap in the market where a company can make money

scarcity When there are not enough goods and services to satisfy the wants and needs of the consumer

sponsors People or companies who wish to be associated with an event by investing money

supply and demand A basic economic theory in which the demand (wants) of the consumer drives the supply (production) of a product

trade-off The choice made to give up one thing to afford another, due to the fact that their resources (money) are limited

union An organization created to represent the collective interests of a particular group of skilled laborers

varied expenses The monthly expenses in a budget that change from month to month such as groceries, transportation, and electricity

VIP Very Important Person

yield Income returned on an investment

FIND OUT MORE

BOOKS TO READ

Acton, Johnny, and David Goldblatt. *Eyewitness Books: Economy.* Dorling Kindersley, 2010.

Andrews, Carolyn. *What Are Goods and Services?* (Economics in Action). Crabtree Publishing, 2008.

Challen, Paul. *What Is Supply and Demand?* (Economics in Action). Crabtree Publishing, 2010.

Flatt, Lizann. *The Economics of the Super Bowl* (Economics of Entertainment). Crabtree Publishing, 2013.

Girard Golomb, Kristen. *Economics and You, Grades 5–8.* Mark Twain Media, 2012.

Hollander, Barbara. *Money Matters: An Introduction to Economics.* Heinemann Raintree, 2010.

Hulick, Kathryn. *The Economics of a Video Game* (Economics of Entertainment). Crabtree Publishing, 2013.

Johnson, Robin. *The Economics of Making a Movie* (Economics of Entertainment). Crabtree Publishing, 2013.

WEBSITES

http://dailyinfographic.com
Information of all types presented visually

www.billboard.com
Facts, figures, and news about the music industry

www.scholastic.com/browse/collection.jsp?id=455
Articles and activities about the economy

www.socialstudiesforkids.com/subjects/economics.htm
An overview of economics

www.the-numbers.com
Box office data and records

INDEX

REFERENCES

ACKNOWLEDGMENTS
The author wishes to thank the following people for assistance and credit these sources of information:

Books
Flynn, Sean, Ph.D. *Economics for Dummies.* Hoboken: Wiley Publishing, Inc., 2nd Edition, 2011.

Klein, Grady, and Yoram Bauman, Ph.D. *The Cartoon Introduction to Economics: Volume One: Microeconomics.* New York: D & M Publishers, Inc., 2010.

Larson, Jennifer S. *Who's Buying? Who's Selling?: Understanding Consumers and Producers.* Minneapolis: Lerner Publishing, Inc., 2010.

Larson, Jennifer S. *What Can You Do with Money?: Earning, Spending, and Saving.* Minneapolis: Lerner Publishing, Inc., 2010.

Waddell, Ray D., Rich Barnet, and Jake Berry. *This Business of Concert Promotion and Touring: A Practical Guide to Creating, Selling, Organizing, and Staging Concerts.* Crown Publishing Group, 2007.

Wolfe, Leonard. *Easy Economics: A Visual Guide to What You Need to Know.* Hoboken: John Wiley & Sons, Inc., 2012.

Websites
www.socialstudiesforkids.com/subjects/economicsbasic.htm

http://kids.usa.gov/money

www.vrml.k12.la.us/cc/economics/economics.htm

Industry Reports and Articles
"Aerosmith Concert... Behind the Scenes," *Today Show,* 2004.

"Average Ticket Prices," Pollstar, 2013.

Chace, Zoe. "How Much Does It Cost To Make A Hit Song?" Planet Money, June 30, 2011.

"The Concert-Tour Economy," *Newsweek,* June 5, 2011.

Economics Vocabulary, Teacher Created Resources, Inc.

Etu. "Economist Alan Krueger examines pricing of concert tickets," News at Princeton, September 24, 2002.

Firecloud, Johnny. "Top 10 Highest Grossing Tours of All Time," Crave Online, August 9, 2012.

Krueger, Alan B. *The Economics of Real Superstars: The Market for Rock Concerts in the Material World,* April 12, 2004.

Plummer, Robert. "Winners take all in rockonomics," *BBC News,* April 20, 2006.

Rabhan, Jeff. "Music Industry Predictions: Labels, Concerts, Licensing and More," Reverbnation, January 31, 2013.

Tanners, Jon. "Fascinating Music Industry Stats," Pigeons and Planes, December 7, 2012.

"10 Interesting Facts about the World's Most Famous Arena," USA Student Travel, April, 20, 2011.

Vie, Ryo. "The Price Of A Concert: Breaking Down Where The Money Goes," The Rock and Roll Guru, March 20, 2011.

Physical Science

Hands-On Activities to Promote Student Involvement

by
Frank White

illustrated by Veronica Terrill

Cover by Ted Warren

Copyright © 1993, Good Apple

ISBN No. 0-86653-725-2

Printing No. 987654321

Good Apple
1204 Buchanan St., Box 299
Carthage, IL 62321-0299

S I M O N & S C H U S T E R *A Paramount Communications Company*

Dedication

What we have to learn to do, we learn by doing.

Aristotle

Dedicated to those kids who ask, "Why not ?"

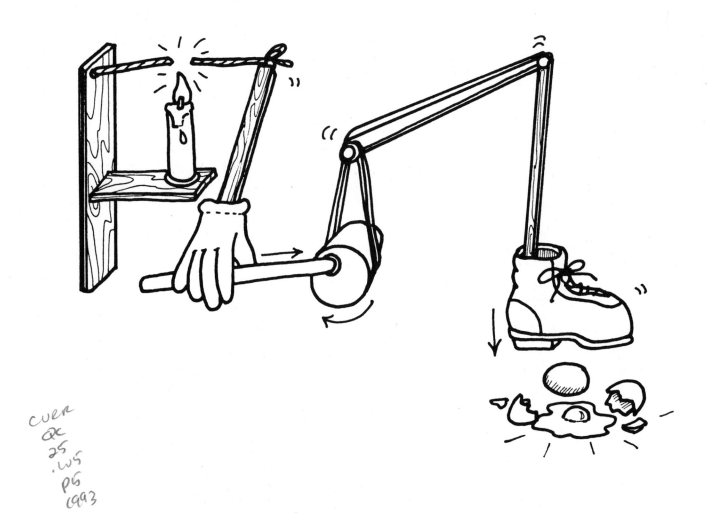

Table of Contents

Chemistry

Magnetism

Electricity

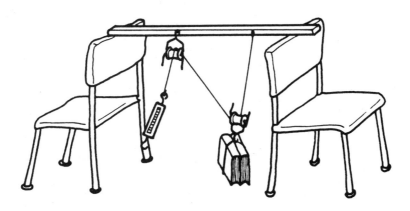

GA1444

Light

Pressures

Sound

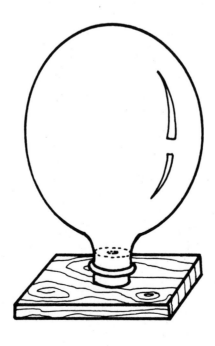

GA1444

Machines

Additional Fun Projects

Teacher Support

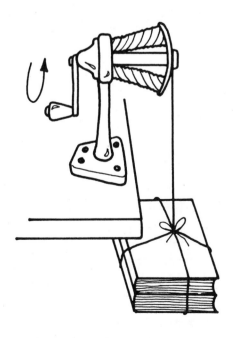

Preface

This book is designed to place science investigation in the hands of the students. Learning becomes more concrete and concepts mastered more fully when learning is interactive. *Science* means "experimentation," and it should be kept in mind that the manipulation of materials with a goal is as important at this stage of scientific investigation as a "successful" outcome.

The book has been divided into teacher background information and projects. The teacher background information is designed to give the scientifically less experienced teacher a short introduction in the "science" of the project and provide a short overview about the projects. The projects are divided into student projects and teacher/student projects. The student projects are designed as class-wide projects, and it is suggested that students be allowed to work together in small groups of three or four. Some student projects may be completed at home and returned the following day.

The teacher/student projects are designed to be completed by the teacher with student help and input. The tendency to "do" for the students should be avoided. At every opportunity let the students measure, pour, mix, categorize, cut, tie, weigh, and most of all discuss and be led to ask questions about the projects. The opportunity for in-depth, scientific understanding and appreciation exists within these pages, but only your enthusiasm and interest can bring science to life.

Science often requires more different kinds of materials than any other subject area. While an effort was made to keep the material requirements to a minimum, certain materials are musts. The teacher should feel free to make substitutions if necessary. As an example, a large glass jar may work instead of an expensive aquarium.

Have the students play an active role in supplying the necessary materials for projects. When the students bring in science supplies, they are providing more than the materials. They are coming to class prepared with a positive attitude about "their" science projects.

A positive attitude and genuine interest will pay far greater dividends in a child's education than learning a given scientific fact. A fact may provide a specific answer, but attitude, interest and an inquiring mind will provide the questions, and questions are the driving force in science.

Chemistry

A study of physical science can begin with the study of atoms. Everything and everyone is made up of atoms. Your desk and chair, this book, and even the ink on the paper are composed of atoms. Atoms are so tiny that they can only be seen through the most powerful electron microscopes.

A model of an atom can be visualized by thinking of an atom as a miniature solar system. The nucleus of an atom would be represented by the sun with the electron corresponding to the plants. The three most familiar atomic particles, electrons, neutrons, and protons, have some relative characteristics that may be difficult for the students to grasp. The electrons orbit the nucleus at such fantastic speeds that they can complete billions of trips in a millionth of a second. A proton is about 2000 times heavier than an electron. If an electron were the weight of a 75-pound (33.75 kg) child, the neutrons and protons would each weigh as much as fifty automobiles.

Most of an atom is composed of space. If an atom's nucleus was increased to the size of a marble (a gigantic size change), some of the electrons (depending on the atom) would be 50 yards (45.5 m) away and smaller than a BB.

These distances, sizes, and speeds need to be put in "kid terms." If a student could travel as fast as an electron, he could make the trip from school to home to school several million times in one second. If the students were the size of a proton or neutron, they could easily have everyone in their state, holding hands, spread out and still easily pass through the eye of a needle.

The atom also contains other important parts. Other nucleus particles include neutrinos, mesons, hyperons, and antiparticles to name a few. At this level of study it is generally sufficient to say they exist. Some of these particles are so short-lived that their life span is measured in hundred billionths and hundred trillionths of a second.

Groups of chemical substances (composed of atoms) are either elements or compounds. Oxygen and hydrogen are elements, whereas water is a compound composed of oxygen and hydrogen.

An interesting educational activity is the building of molecular models to represent common compounds. Scientists use a one or two-letter symbol for each of the over one hundred different elements. They use these symbols to write formulas for compounds. Hydrogen is represented by an H, oxygen by an O, and the compound water has the formula H_2O to illustrate that a molecule of water has two hydrogen atoms to one oxygen atom. Using colored marshmallows to represent the elements and toothpicks to represent the bonds that hold them together, give the students an excellent understanding of how a molecule is constructed.

Student Project 1

GA1444

The marshmallows can be eaten after the project is completed, but be sure to remind the students that this is one of a few projects that is safe to eat. (Small pieces of carrot, celery, potato, beet, etc., can be substituted for colored marshmallows.)

Children like to see the reaction of different substances. The old standby baking soda and vinegar reaction can be extended to make macaroni "dance." When baking soda mixes with vinegar, the foaming result demonstrates the production of carbon dioxide (CO_2). With the dancing macaroni project, the CO_2 attaches to the macaroni, making it lighter than the water mixture and causing it to rise. When the macaroni reaches the surface, the CO_2 bubbles burst and the macaroni once again sinks. This reaction (RXN) will continue for over an hour and can even be prolonged by the addition of more baking soda and vinegar.

Student Project 2

Teacher/Student Project 1

GA1444

Several other simple, yet educational, chemical and physical reactions are appropriate to study at this time.

A raw egg (with the shell intact) placed in vinegar will become so rubbery that within a week it will bounce. The acetic acid in vinegar will dissolve the calcium shell and react with the protein to become rubber-like to survive a drop of several inches (centimeters).

A common nail placed in a bottle of soda pop will dissolve over time. The same result will occur if you place a tooth in a bottle of soda pop. This is a very powerful demonstration and can lead into a good discussion of nutrition.

Steel wool can be burned with the heat of a candle flame. This physical reaction demonstrates the need for oxygen for combustion.

Teacher/Student Project 2   Teacher/Student Project 3   Teacher/Student Project 4

Crystals

Living things, from begonias to blue whales, grow from seeds or eggs. Many nonliving substances, such as salt, ice, and minerals are produced by a process of crystallization.

Growing crystals is a fascinating way to demonstrate reactions. Crystals may be grown from several household substances: salt, sugar, and a combination of ammonia, salt, and laundry bluing. Other more colorful crystals can be "grown" using copper sulfate (blue), ammonium dichromate (orange) and nickel sulfate (green). Each solution must be saturated or unable to dissolve any additional material. Warm water will dissolve more of a given chemical than will cold water. Often crystal growing can be a slow process. The process can be speeded up, knowing the effects of heated water and saturation. Using a watch glass and boiling water saturated with Epsom salts or alum (both available at most drugstores), crystals can be seen growing as the water begins to cool. The clear watch glass can be placed on an overhead projector (or projection microscope) and projected on a screen for everyone to see as a greatly enlarged picture.

Student Project 3

Student Project 4

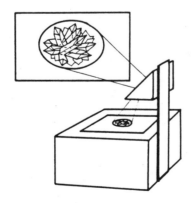

Teacher/Student Project 5

Acids and Bases

Acids and bases can be studied at the elementary level with great success using some readily available materials. The students will already be familiar with some acids without knowing it. Formic acid gives ants their distinctive smell, citric acid gives lemons, oranges, and limes their sour taste, while tartaric acid is found in grapes, malic acid in apples, and acetic acid in vinegar. These are all organic acids (acids containing carbon atoms).

The four most recognizable inorganic acids (without carbon atoms) are sulfuric acid, hydrochloric acid, nitric acid, and phosphoric acid. Some of these inorganics are quite strong. They are used mostly in the manufacture of plastics, textiles, certain metals, explosives, and dyes.

Bases are generally considered compounds that react with acids to form salts. Two of the more common bases, sodium hydroxide (household bleach) and ammonium hydroxide (household ammonia) are useful cleaning agents. Because of these atomic structural differences (their affinity to gather or give up hydrogen ions), we can measure the strength of an acid or a base by a number of different tests. Two of the easiest tests are the use of an acid or a base by a number of different tests. Two of the easiest tests are the use of litmus paper and red cabbage juice. Acids turn blue litmus paper red while bases turn red litmus paper blue. The effect of acids and bases on purple cabbage juice can be used as a graphic example of chemical reactions. Acidic solutions turn cabbage juice red while basic solutions react with cabbage juice to turn it green.

Solution	Effect on Pink Litmus Paper	Effect on Blue Litmus Paper	Acid	Base
tap water				
distilled water				
milk				
orange juice				
bleach				
ammonia				
margarine				
coffee				
soda pop				
unknown				
other				
other				

Student Project 5
*suggested unknown solution
yellow food coloring in vinegar

Solution	RXN with Purple Cabbage Juice	Acid	Base	Neutral
tap water				
distilled water				
orange juice				
bleach				
milk				
soda pop				
vinegar				
unknown				
other				
other				

Student Project 6
*suggested unknown solution
yellow food coloring in bleach

Cabbage Juice Indicator Recipe

To make a purple cabbage juice indicator, cut up half of a head of purple cabbage into small pieces and boil fifteen minutes in four cups (960 ml) of water. Pour liquid into another container and let it cool. You may need to further dilute the juice with another two cups (480 ml) of water. Too concentrated a solution will not yield a good indicator.

Teacher's Note: This lesson is best accomplished using stations. After explaining the procedures and discussing any questions, allow the students to work in small groups and move from station to station to collect their data. (*Suggestion for the "unknown" solution is given above.)

 GA1444

Marshmallow Molecules

Student Project 1

Scientists use one or two-letter symbols to abbreviate the names of different elements. Of the over 100 elements, you have probably heard of some of them such as gold, silver, oxygen, hydrogen, helium, mercury, copper, chlorine, lead, and nitrogen to name a few.

We will use colored marshmallows to represent certain elements and toothpicks to represent the bonds, or forces, that hold them together. When we combine the elements in very specific ways, we will create a model of a specific compound. Before we begin, here are some definitions.

- **Atom:** The smallest particle of matter with specific chemical characteristics (having electrons, protons, neutrons).

- **Element:** A substance that cannot be broken down into a simpler substance. (Oxygen, gold, and hydrogen are elements.)

- **Compound:** A chemical combination of two or more elements. (Water is a compound.)

- **Molecule:** The smallest particle into which a substance can be divided and still remain like the original substance. (A single water molecule [H_2O] contains two hydrogen atoms and one oxygen atom.)

Materials:
several miniature white and colored marshmallows
toothpicks

Use the following chart to build model molecules:

Element	Symbol	Color of Marshmallow
Hydrogen	H	white
Oxygen	O	yellow
Carbon	C	green
Nitrogen	N	pink

Compound	Chemical Formula	# Hydrogen Molecules	# Oxygen Molecules	# Carbon Molecules	# Nitrogen Molecules
Water	H_2O	2	1	0	0
Carbon dioxide	CO_2	0	2	1	0
Ammonia	NH_3	3	0	0	1
Carbon monoxide	CO	0	1	1	0

Use the space below to draw, label, and color what your models looked like.

A drop of water contains 33,000,000,000,000,000,000 molecules.

Name _____

Date _____

Simple Reactions

Student Project 2

This project shows a dramatic reaction that occurs when two specific chemicals are mixed.

Materials:
    a large glass or beaker
    3-4 tbs. (45-60 ml) of vinegar
    1 tbs. (15 ml) baking soda
    paper towels (just in case)

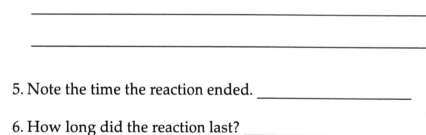

Procedure:
    1. Note the time. _____

    2. Pour the vinegar in the glass.

    3. Add the baking soda.

    4. Describe the reaction.

_____

_____

_____

    5. Note the time the reaction ended. _____

    6. How long did the reaction last? _____

* Remember: *Never* **mix together any unknown substances!**

---

baking soda + vinegar   =   *carbon dioxide* (CO_2)

GA1444

Dancing Macaroni

Teacher/Student Project 1

The production of carbon dioxide (CO_2) gas by the mixing of vinegar and baking soda was demonstrated in Student Project 2. We can make dancing macaroni by using this information.

Materials:
    a very large, *clear* glass or plastic container (A one-gallon clear water bottle works
        well.)
    box of baking soda
    bottle of white vinegar
    water
    20-30 small, dry macaroni or spaghetti pieces

Procedure:
    1. Fill the container half full of water.

    2. Add half a bottle of vinegar.

    3. Add 5-6 tablespoons (75-90 ml) of baking soda. (Add very, very slowly.)

    4. Add the macaroni.

Although exact proportions are not essential, some modification of proportions may be necessary to achieve the optimum effect.

Discussion Question:
    Why does the macaroni continue to move up and down?

GA1444

Bouncing Eggs

Teacher/Student Project 2

A chicken's egg is enclosed by a shell that has a high calcium content. If a raw egg (shell still intact) is placed in a glass of vinegar, a reaction (RXN) takes place. The acetic acid in the vinegar will dissolve the eggshell and the egg will bounce.

The reaction will begin immediately when the egg is placed in the vinegar but will not be complete for two or three days. After two or three days, the egg will survive a drop of four or five inches (10.16 or 12.7 cm).

Competition Idea:
Have each student begin the project at home on Monday and see whose egg will survive a fall from the highest distance on Friday.

Dissolving a Nail

Teacher/Student Project 3

A small, plain nail can be dissolved by soda pop. Place a small nail in a bottle of soda pop and observe the results over several weeks. This reaction is slower than the reaction of the dissolving eggshell in Teacher/Student Project 2. This reaction requires more time. You may wish to substitute a tooth for the nail and record the results. Try several different objects and compare their rates of reaction.

GA1444

Burning Steel

Teacher/Student Project 4

Almost any material will burn if it gets hot enough and there is enough oxygen for combustion. Coal mine explosions often occur because coal dust (very fine particles) in the air is easily ignited by a spark or an open flame. Even steel will burn if heated hot enough. Using tongs, hold a small piece of steel wool (very fine threads of steel) in a candle flame. Observe the results.

As an extension of this idea, it is possible to boil water in a paper cup by suspending a small cup half filled with water over a candle flame. Since the paper will burn at about 451°F (232.77°C) and water boils at 212°F (100°C), the heat will cause the water to boil before the paper cup burns.

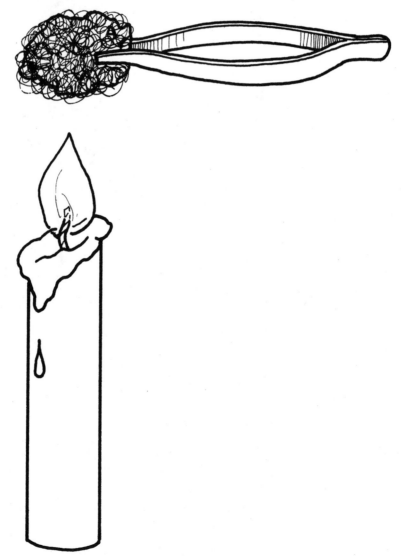

12

GA1444

Crystal Gardens

Student Project 3

Most of the earth's crust is composed mainly of crystals. Diamonds, granite, coal, and quartz are all examples of natural crystals called minerals. They are formed by dissolved salts in the water in the earth's crust and left undisturbed by long periods of time or by the crystallization of magma (molten lava under the surface) under tremendous heat and pressure.

You can grow your own crystals from simple household materials.

Materials:

ammonia   assorted food colorings
salt   aluminium pie plate
laundry bluing   water
small charcoal briquettes or broken bits of red brick

Procedure:

1. In a glass or beaker, mix together 5 tablespoons (75 ml) of water, 5 tablespoons (75 ml) of salt, 2 tablespoons (30 ml) of ammonia, and 1 tablespoon (15 ml) of laundry bluing.

2. Place several pieces of broken up bricks or charcoal in the bottom of the pie pan and pour the solution over it.

3. Place one or two drops of food coloring on the briquettes.

4. Put the pan in a place where it will be undisturbed for several days but can still be watched. As the water evaporates, the salts will grow in interesting crystal formations.

5. Use a hand lens to observe the crystal garden. On the back of this page illustrate what your crystals look like.

Diamond is the hardest, naturally occurring substance known to man.

Name _____

Date _____

Growing Crystals

Student Project 4

Crystallization is a physical change. It accounts for most of the material in the earth's crust. It is the process that creates snowflakes, ice cubes, table salt, coal, and diamonds.

To grow crystals you will need to understand some basic concepts and terms.

• *Saturation* means "no more material can be dissolved in the solution."

• A warm or hot solution will dissolve more material than a cold solution.

Materials:

hot plate
small, clear plastic glasses
plastic spoon (for stirring)
water
one of the following chemicals:

heat-safe beaker or small pan
cotton string
pencil or doweling that will
    reach across top of plastic glass

Chemical	Color
salt	clear
sugar	clear
alum	clear
ammonium dichromate	orange
copper sulfate	blue
nickel sulfate	green

Caution:

Copper sulfate, ammonium dichromate, and nickel sulfate are all very dangerous chemicals, and great care should be used when handling them. Make sure an adult is always present to supervise their use.

Procedure:

In a beaker or small saucepan bring $\frac{1}{4}$ cup (60 ml) water to a boil. Take the container off the hot plate and slowly add your selected chemical and stir until it's dissolved. Continue adding and stirring in your material until the solution is saturated and no more material will dissolve. Pour your solution into the plastic glass. Cut a string long enough to be tied to the pencil or doweling and still reach the solution. Place your project in an undisturbed place where you can observe your crystals growing. As the water evaporates, your crystals will increase in size.

Always wash your hands after touching this project.

Emeralds, which are crystals, are the birthstones for the month of May.

GA1444

Crystal Formation Observation

Teacher/Student Project 5

The following experiment illustrates how crystals can be formed.

Materials:
   watch glass (a clear petri dish or a pane of glass will also work)
   warmed, saturated solution of alum or Epsom salts
   overhead projector
   small paintbrush

Procedure:
   Mix a two-tablespoon (30 ml) saturated solution of alum or Epsom salts. Place a thin layer of the solution on a watch glass, petri dish, or pane of glass. As the water evaporates, crystals will begin to form. Display your project on an overhead projector for the class to see in its greatly enlarged form. Illustrate the resulting crystals on construction paper and label.

   This project may also be done with a regular microscope or projection microscope. Solutions of salt or sugar can be used when magnified.

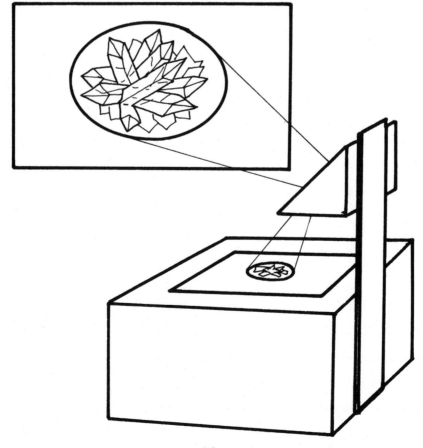

Name _____

Date _____

Acid-Base Tests

Student Project 5

The use of litmus paper is the most common way to test a solution for the presence of an acid or a base. Two colors of litmus paper, pink and blue, are used. The intensity of color change can be used to determine to what degree a solution is acidic or basic. *Acids turn pink litmus paper blue, and bases turn blue litmus paper pink.* Use this information to determine if the solutions in the table are acidic or basic.

Materials:

    pink and blue litmus paper
    plastic cups or petri dishes containing the solutions listed in the table (clearly marked)

Procedure:

    Carefully dip the litmus paper $1/4$" (.6 cm) into the solution and note the results. Be careful not to get your finger in the various substances.

Solution	Effect on Pink Litmus Paper	Effect on Blue Litmus Paper	Acid	Base
tap water				
distilled water				
milk				
orange juice				
bleach				
ammonia				
margarine				
coffee				
soda pop				
unknown				
other				
other				

Tannic acid from the bark of certain trees was used by the pioneers to tan and preserve furs.

GA1444

Acids and Bases

Student Project 6

Red cabbage juice can be used as an acid-base indicator. Acids will turn purple cabbage juice red and bases will turn purple cabbage juice green.

Materials:
  $1/2$ cup (120 ml) of several different liquids
  clear plastic cups
  purple cabbage juice indicator

Procedure:
  Pour $1/4$ cup (60 ml) cabbage juice into a clear plastic cup. Add 2-3 tablespoons (30-45 ml) of the solution to be checked to the juice and note the results.

Solution	RXN with Purple Cabbage Juice	Acid	Base	Neutral
tap water				
distilled water				
orange juice				
bleach				
milk				
soda pop				
vinegar				
unknown				
other				
other				

GA1444

Magnetism

Magnetism is a subject of great interest to students. Its unseen force spurs inquiry and interest. A magnet behaves as it does because of the arrangement of the atoms in the material. Each atom has a north and south polarity and is generally arranged in no definite order. When a piece of iron is magnetized, millions of the atoms align with their north poles pointing in one direction and their south poles pointing in the opposite direction. The more atoms that align this way, the stronger the magnet.

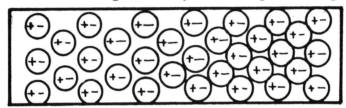

Magnetism has been known of since the beginning of written history. Some early men knew of magnetism because of lodestones. These magnetic rocks were believed to have special powers and were used even up into the Middle Ages for medicinal purposes.

You can magnetize a needle by rubbing it forty to fifty times (in the same direction) with a magnet. Apply petroleum jelly to your new "magnetic" needle, float it in a paper cup filled with water and you have a compass. You can set up an interesting demonstration by taping a magnet to a ruler and "suspending" a paper clip held by thread. If several magnets with holes in them are available, a demonstration of "floating magnets" can be made for the students. All of these demonstration projects can be lifted out for the student's use.

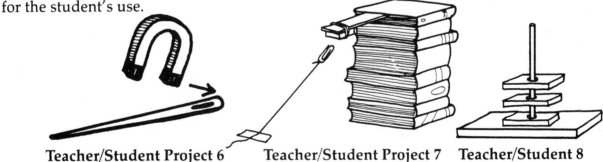

Teacher/Student Project 6   **Teacher/Student Project 7**   **Teacher/Student 8**

Students will enjoy determining the magnetism of various materials. After the projects, the students should be able to relate that only metals containing iron or steel are magnetic (ferrous metals). This concept can be extended to state that magnetic fields can only pass through non-ferrous metals. Let the students experiment to see which materials (wood, copper, steel, etc.) will allow magnetic fields to pass through them and which will not.

Material	Hypothesis yes	no	Actual yes	no
brass paper fastener				
piece of chalk				
aluminum can				
nail				
penny				
nickel				
quarter				
pencil				
gold ring				
paper clip				
other				
other				

Student Project 7

Magnetizing a Needle;
Suspending Paper Clips; Floating Magnets

Teacher/Student Projects 6, 7 and 8

Magnetizing a Needle–Project 6

Stroke a magnet forty to fifty times (always in the same direction) across the end of a needle and carefully place it in a paper or plastic cup. Presto: Instant compass.

Suspending Paper Clips–Project 7

Taping a magnet to a ruler and using a thread to suspend a paper clip will demonstrate invisible magnetic fields.

Floating Magnets–Project 8

Magnets with holes in them can be used to demonstrate the levitation effect that may be used on transportation of the future.

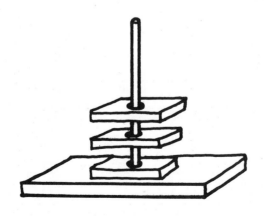

GA1444

Name _____

Date _____

Magnetic Objects

Student Project 7

Magnets do not attract all objects. Determine the characteristics which make an object magnetic. Before you conduct your experiment, hypothesize (make an educated guess) which objects will be attracted to a magnet.

Material	Hypothesis		Actual	
	yes	no	yes	no
brass paper fastener				
piece of chalk				
aluminum can				
nail				
penny				
nickel				
quarter				
pencil				
gold ring				
paper clip				
other				
other				
other				
other				

What statement can you make about those items attracted to the magnet?

_____

_____

_____

The magnetic properties of materials were first explained by the French scientist André Ampère.

GA1444

Electricity

The simplest experiment of determining what materials conduct electricity is a good project for the students to start on. Making a circuit continuity tester is a useful project should the students decide to complete extra circuit activities.

Electricity is a form of energy. In its simplest idea, electricity can be thought of as the flow of electrons. Electricity is the most useable form of energy. It provides us with heat, light, power, radio, television, telephone and time (clocks). From computers to can openers, electricity is a part of our everyday lives. Students can list all the uses of electricity on the chalkboard as a good introduction to the uses of electricity.

There are several good electrical projects the students will enjoy. With a battery, a short length of insulated wire, a nail and a rubber band, the students can make a simple working electromagnet. Add a couple of paper clips, two magnets, and some enamelled wire, and the students can build a fine example of an electric motor.

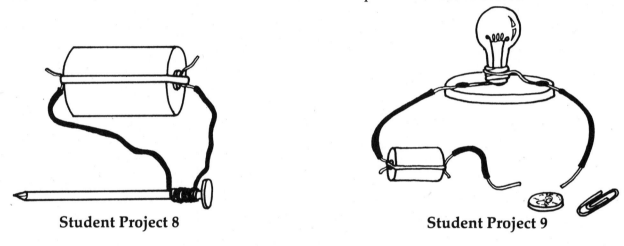

Student Project 8   **Student Project 9**

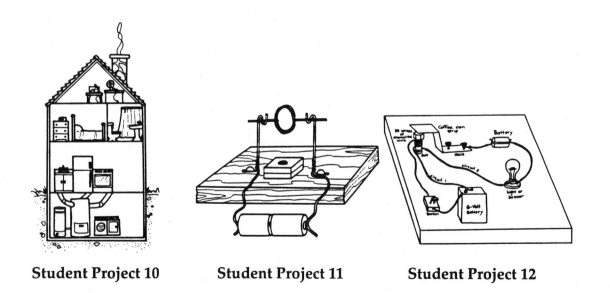

Student Project 10   **Student Project 11**   **Student Project 12**

GA1444

Building Electromagnets

Student Project 8

When electricity travels in a circle, a magnetic field is generated down the center of the circle of electricity. This fact can be used to turn a nail into a magnet.

Wrap 18" (45.72 cm) of insulated #18-#20 bell wire around a nail. Strip 1" (2.54 cm) of the insulation from each end of the wire. *Be careful. If you hold the wires directly to the battery, the wires will become very hot.* Use a rubber band to hold the wire to the battery. The electricity travelling through the wire will create a magnetic field that will magnetize the nail, turning it into a magnet. See how many paper clips your electromagnet will pick up. Try various combinations of batteries and wraps of wire around the nail to see if you can create a more and more powerful electromagnet. Record your results on the chart on the following page.

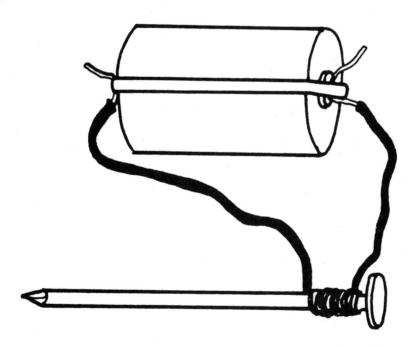

Note: Always wrap the wire from the head of the nail toward the point.

Voltage	# of Wraps of Wire	# of Rows of Wrapped Wire	# of Paper Clips Picked Up

What generalization can you make about an electromagnet's power relative to voltage, number of wraps of wire and number of rows of wraps?

_____

_____

_____

In 1820, Christian Oersted of Denmark discovered electromagnetism by holding a compass near a wire carrying an electrical current.

Materials That Conduct Electricity

Student Project 9

What materials conduct electricity? Are there materials that conduct electricity better than others? Set up the simple test apparatus as illustrated below and conduct your own test to determine those materials that conduct electricity.

Set up the test apparatus so contact of the wires will cause the light bulb to come on. Place the various materials, one at a time, between the wire contacts and record whether or not the light lights up. For the solutions, place the wires in the solutions, not touching each other, and record the results in the chart on the following page.

Building a Continuity Tester

Material	Expected Results	Actual Results
copper wire		
penny		
aluminum foil		
nickel		
rubber band		
cup of soda pop		
cup of distilled water		
cup of salt water		
nail		
pencil lead		
glass		
plastic		
other		
other		

Discussion Questions:
1. What do the objects or solutions that conduct electricity have in common?
2. What other objects do you think conduct electricity?
3. What other objects will not conduct electricity?
4. Define *insulation*.

About 3,000,000,000,000,000,000 electrons flow past a single point in an electric light bulb every second.

GA1444

Electric Motors (uses)

Student Project 10

Electric motors are machines that change electric energy into mechanical power. Electrical motors have thousands of uses and applications. In industry and transportation, electric motors run machines of all types, carry millions of people daily in subways and trollies, move materials by diesel-electric trains, and make it possible to have the kind of society we have.

In our homes, electric motors in clocks, refrigerators, VCR's, washers, dryers, fans, air conditioners, and electric hair dryers are some of the uses to which we put electric motors.

Using the drawing of the house at the right as an example and adding other items not shown, list as many items as you can that use electric motors. Use the back of this paper for your list.

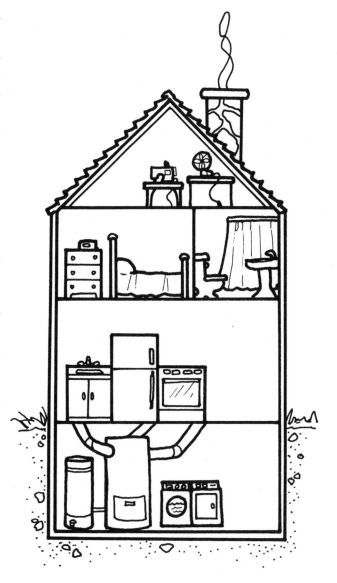

The electric motor attached to your house or apartment measures the amount of electricity your family uses. It was invented in 1888 by Oliver Shallenberger.

GA1444

Name _____

Date _____

Electric Motors (building)

Student Project 11

You can build a working model of a real electric motor. All electric motors are built on three basic principles:

1. Electricity can produce a magnetic field.
2. Like poles on magnets repel each other while opposite poles attract.
3. The direction the current flows determines an electromagnet's polarity.

Build an electric motor.

Materials:
   2 "D" cell, $1\frac{1}{2}$ volt batteries (flashlight batteries)
   2 paper clips
   $6\frac{1}{2}$ feet (1.95 m) enamelled copper wire (#20 wire)
   2 small magnets
   6 thumbtacks
   pliers
   2 12" (30.48 cm) pieces of insulated wire
   small scrap of wood for a base (Paper clips can be taped to a desk, but a wooden base allows the project to be taken home.)
   small piece of sandpaper

Procedure:
   1. Straighten out and rebend the paper clips as illustrated.

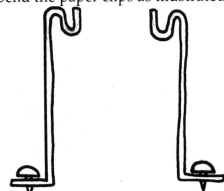

   2. Use the thumbtacks to permanently mount the paper clips approximately 2" to $2\frac{1}{2}$" (5.08 to 6.33 cm) apart.

3. Using the battery as a template, wrap the enameled wire around the battery fifteen to twenty times. Leave enough wire to wrap around the coil so it will be held in a round shape.

4. Use sandpaper to carefully and completely remove the enamel from the end of the wire.

5. Adjust your coil so it is evenly balanced and has no "heavy side."

6. Attach, with insulated wires, your batteries to the paper clips.

7. Place two magnets between the paper clips.

8. Place your coil (armature) on the paper clips.

9. Adjust your coil for level and balance, and adjust the position of the magnets until your motor spins.

 GA1444

Relays

Student Project 12

An electromagnetic relay switch is a challenging project. When completed, two independent electrical circuits will become interdependent, allowing one circuit to activate the other.

Materials:
>   a piece of wood the size of a sheet of paper
> $1/4$" (.6 cm) bolt, 2" (5.08 cm) long, with nuts
>   electric drill with $1/4$" (.6 cm) drill bit
>   strip of thin, bendable metal (coffee can strip) 6-8" (15.24–20.32 cm) long and $1/2$"
>   (1.25 cm) wide
> $1 1/2$ volt "D" cell battery and holder
> $1 1/2$ volt light and holder
>   6-volt lantern type battery
>   approximately 4 feet (1.22 m) of insulated bell wire
>   3 roofing nails

Construct the relay as illustrated.

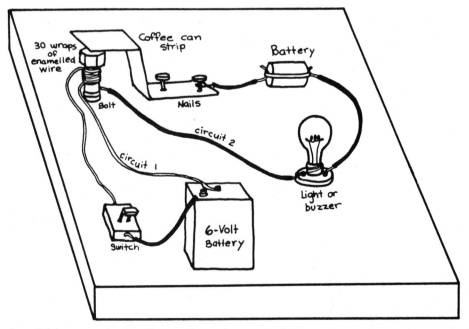

The circuits should be constructed so when the switch is activated on circuit 1, the flow of electricity will create an electromagnetic bolt. This electromagnet will pull on the coffee can strip, completing circuit 2 and light the bulb.

This relay can also be used as a practice key for Morse code.

GA1444

Light

Light may seem to be something so common the students may at first ask, "Why study light?" A short discussion with the students regarding what our life would be like without light, what light gives us and the different kinds of light and its complexity will quickly dispel the notions that light is simple.

Without light there would be no food production because green plants use sunlight to grow and produce food. All the food we eat comes from plants or animals which eat plants. Plants also produce oxygen as they grow, and oxygen is necessary in the air we breathe. Sunlight heats up the earth. Ancient sunlight energy stored as fossil fuels of coal, oil, and natural gas are used to heat and light our homes and schools today.

Light occurs in many different forms. Sunlight, firelight, lamplight, the light of a firefly or pelagic fish, laser light, the Northern Lights, ultraviolet light, and black light are some with which the students may be familiar.

Light is composed of bundles of energy called photons. As an atom is energized or "excited," these bundles are released as the atom progresses to its original level. The higher the level of "excitement" an atom achieves, the higher the level of photon that is released as the atom returns to its regular state. These different levels of excitement account for light of different colors. A very excited atom may release several different photons of different energy levels which allow for an atom's ability to produce several different colors of light. With visible light the photons with the highest levels of energy produce blue light and the least energetic photons produce red light.

It is important for the student to know that in discussing light we are discussing produced light, not reflected light. A green sweater doesn't produce green light but is just a reflection of light. To determine if something produces or reflects light, one must only ask the question, "Could you see it in a completely dark room?" (You could see a candle's light but not an extinguished candle.)

To understand how light behaves there are three key terms: *reflection*, *refraction*, and *absorption*. A ray of light striking an object may be reflected (bounced back), refracted (passed through), or absorbed by the object. The way different materials reflect, refract, and absorb each different wavelength of light gives different objects their color. When white light (for example, from a regular light bulb or sunlight) falls on a colored surface, we see only certain parts of the spectrum. The pretty red sweater a student may be wearing will reflect the red and absorb the other colors of the spectrum, thus it looks red.

Several interesting projects can be used to study light and color. These projects, with appropriate discussion, will lead students to realize the complexity of light as well as its diversity and usefulness. A pencil placed at an angle in a glass of water will demonstrate how different materials affect light waves.

A plastic or glass prism will refract the different light wavelengths to form a spectrum of color (a rainbow). This shows how different wavelengths (colors) are "bent" (actually slowed down) as they pass from one medium to another (air–glass–air).

Teacher/Student Project 9

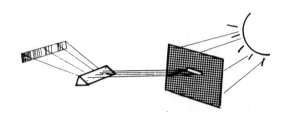

Teacher/Student Project 10

A Benham's Disk has only black and white markings but appears colored when spun (an optical illusion but fun).

Student Project 13

Making colored glasses using various colors of acetate or plastic is an eye-opening project to demonstrate reflection, refraction, and absorption.

Having light wave reflection races is a great project that demonstrates not only reflection but the need for cooperation. You can add a couple of interesting twists to these "races" by adding extra obstacles (movable bulletin boards, students sitting on desks) or not allowing discussion among team members.

Making a kaleidoscope is a great culminating activity, but be very careful of sharp edges.

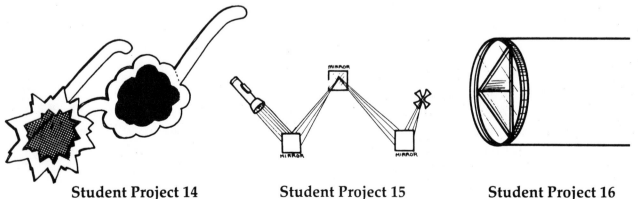

Student Project 14   **Student Project 15**   **Student Project 16**

32

Bending a Pencil

Teacher/Student Project 9

Light rays change their direction as they pass through different transparent substances. This can be observed by completing this simple project.

Place a pencil in a glass of water. Let the pencil rest at an angle. Note the illusion while viewing the pencil from the level it enters the water. The pencil appears bent or broken. This occurs because the light rays reflected from the pencil in the water are bent at a different angle than those traveling in air alone.

Repeat the above project, slowly adding cooking or mineral oil to the water and then placing the pencil in the liquid. What differences do you see? How can you explain the difference?

Prisms and Rainbows

Teacher/Student Project 10

White light is composed of all the colors of the spectrum. As these colors pass through a prism, each one is slowed down at a different rate, causing the colors to separate. This is the same principle that creates rainbows in the sky when the sun comes out after a rain shower. The droplets of moisture in the air act as prisms to refract the light into a rainbow. To demonstrate the rainbow effect caused by a prism, follow this procedure.

Procedure:
1. Find a place where sunlight enters the room.

2. Cut a $1/8$" x 1" (0.31 x 2.54 cm) slit in a black sheet of construction paper or dark cardboard.

3. Place this paper in the sunlight's path.

4. Darken the room as best as possible.

5. Place the prism in the beam of light coming through the slit.

6. Turn the prism until a rainbow is cast on the wall.

If the classroom doesn't have available sunlight, the following options may be used in lieu of sunlight:

• Someone may reflect sunlight from outside to inside the classroom using a large mirror.

• Perform the activity outside, using a cardboard box to "catch" your rainbow.

• Use the lamp from a filmstrip projector as your light source.

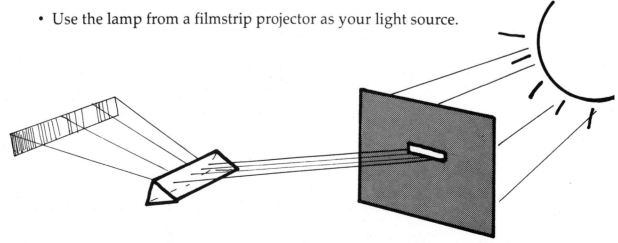

Benham's Disk

Student Project 13

A very interesting illusion of making color where no color existed was demonstrated in 1894 by Charles E. Benham. Narrow black lines placed close together seem to take on color if we stare at them long enough. When moved, they seem to have several colors. If the disk below is spun at a rate of 5-15 revolutions per second (rps), the short, curved lines appear as colored rings. The colors of the rings–red inner, blue outer–will change depending on the direction you spin the disk.

Directions:

Cut out this disk and glue it on an index card or a piece of cardboard. Stick a pin through the center and hold one end as you pin through the center and hold one end as you spin the disk. Remember to try spinning the disk in both directions and record the results.

When spun to the right (clockwise), what were the results? _____

_____

When spun to the left (counterclockwise), what differences could you detect? _____

_____

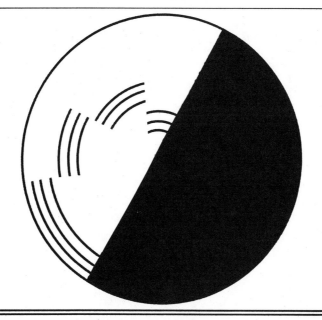

A German psychologist, G.T. Fechner, demonstrated this effect in 1838. . .
called Fechner's Colors.

Out-of-This-World Sunglasses

Student Project 14

When white light shines on an object, some of the light is absorbed and some is reflected or bounced away. Since white light is composed of all the colors of the rainbow, some of the colors may be absorbed and others may be reflected. A red apple absorbs all the light waves except the red ones. A blue ribbon absorbs all the light waves except blue. White objects don't absorb light. Black, on the other hand, absorbs all the wavelengths of light and reflects none. This is the reason a black cat, for instance, looks black.

Directions:

Using colored plastic or acetate, produce your own "out-of-this-world" pair of sunglasses.

Take an out-of-this-world walk with your class and note carefully the colors and feelings you encounter on this walk.

> *When too little light shines on an object, it cannot reflect enough light so our eyes can determine its color. That's why everything looks gray or black in very dim light or at night.*

Light Reflection Relay Race

Student Project 15

A mirror is an almost perfect reflector of light. The angle at which a beam of light strikes a mirror will equal the angle at which the beam is reflected.

Materials:
    a flashlight
    3 mirrors

Knowing this scientific principle and working together in partnership with your teammates, you will "bounce" the light from a flashlight to a specific spot in the least possible time. A sample setup is diagrammed below.

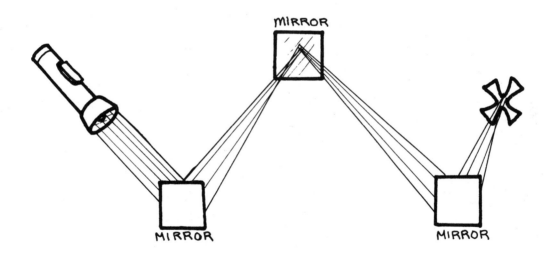

Rules:

1. No teammates may be within "touching distance" of another team member.

2. Time starts when first team member turns on flashlight.

3. Teams may align themselves before they begin.

4. Timing stops when the finish point is illuminated.

5. Every team member must "touch" the light. (No shortcutting a team member.)

Complete the chart below during the competition.

	Group Name	Start Time	Finish Time	Elapsed Time Finish Time –Start Time
1.				
2.				
3.				
4.				
5.				
6.				
7.				
8.				
9.				
10.				

Graph the results.

Elapsed Time

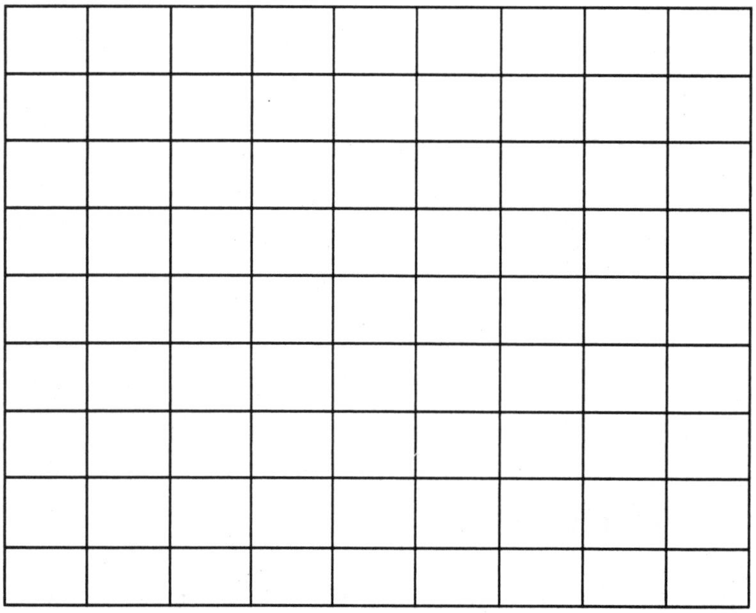

Group Name

The speed of light is 186,282 miles (299,792 kilometers) per second!

GA1444

Name _____

Date _____

Building a Kaleidoscope

Student Project 16

To build a kaleidoscope, you need three 2" wide by 12" long (5.08 x 30.48 cm) mirror pieces, some clear acetate or plastic (see next page), tape, sandpaper, and small bits of bright plastic or paper.

Directions:

1. Sand the mirror pieces on the edges to remove sharp edges. (You may wish to have an adult complete this first step.) Be very careful handling the glass mirror pieces; they are extremely sharp.

2. Tape the mirror pieces together in a triangle, with the mirrored sides facing in.

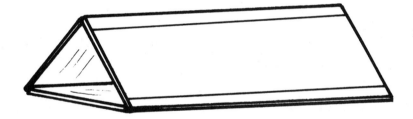

3. Cut out two pieces of clear plastic to fit over the end of the triangle.

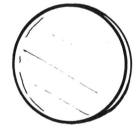

4. Stand kaleidoscope on end.

5. Tape one clear, plastic triangle to the end.

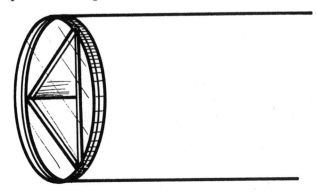

GA1444

6. Place four to five small pieces of bright plastic on top of the clear plastic.

7. Tape second clear, plastic triangle on top of the other plastic triangle, sandwiching bright plastic pieces between. The second plastic triangle should be loose enough to allow the bright plastic pieces to move around freely.

Roll up your kaleidoscope in construction paper in a round shape.

View your kaleidoscope. You should be able to see thousands of different shapes.

Note: The clear plastic container covers that are found in the deli and meat sections of many grocery stores work well. An average lid can provide not only the two triangular pieces, but with some felt tip markers it can make the bright plastic pieces needed.

Sir David Brewster invented the kaleidoscope in the early 1800's.

Pressures

The effects of different kinds of forces can create some dramatic examples of scientific principles. Several projects involving air pressure are an interesting way to begin a study of forces.

Telling the students that they line the bottom of an ocean will stir some discussion. When they decide you're talking about an ocean of air, you're ready to discuss and demonstrate the power of the air around us. If you use as an example the pressure of the blanket of air above us to the pressure you feel when extra blankets are placed on the bed, the concept becomes clear. Most students will also be able to relate to the pressure on your eardrums when you dive to the bottom of a swimming pool. This pressure is due to the "blanket" of water pushing down on you.

The blanket of air above the earth is about 100 miles (160 kilometers) deep. This creates a pressure of approximately 15 pounds per square inch (1 kilogram per square centimeter). These numbers may not make much sense to the students, but a simple experiment with a glass of water and an index card will illustrate the concept.

Teacher/Student Project 11

Once the students start to appreciate the power of air pressure, it is time to bring out your big gun—a dramatic example of air pressure. For this demonstration you will need an empty duplicating fluid or paint thinner can (with cap) and a hot plate. This experiment which entails crushing a can without touching it shows the power of air pressure—a great math follow-up problem of how many pounds of force were applied to the can.

Teacher/Student Project 12

GA1444

A further demonstration of various pressures can be made with a coffee can, a nail, and some water.

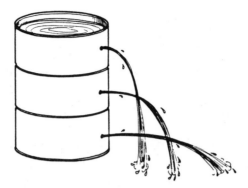

Teacher/Student Project 13

We can also use air pressure to put an egg in a bottle, keep a kite aloft, and build a winning frictionless racer.

Teacher/Student Project 14

Student Project 17

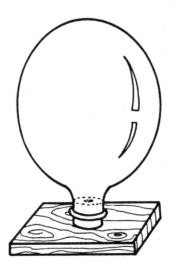

Student Project 18

GA1444

Three fun projects for class competition all use the science of air study as a base. Students can work in cooperative groups of two or three students to create balloon rockets that can be raced against each other. The balloon rockets move using escaping air to generate a force in one direction that propels the rocket in the opposite direction. Giving the students index cards, tape, markers, and other ways of personalizing their racers, will add pizazz to the contest. This is a simple example of Isaac Newton's third law of motion: For every action there is an equal but opposite reaction. Jumping from a stationary skateboard where the rider goes forward and the skateboard "shoots" backward is also a good demonstration of Newton's third law.

Making parachutes is another study of the physics of air resistance. Plastic shopping bags work great, but let the students use any size bag they bring in. The principle remains the same. A slingshot can be used to launch the parachutes or they can simply be rolled up and thrown. Whatever you choose, the "science" remains the same. Resistance (friction) can lead to some good discussions about water resistance (ever try walking fast in a swimming pool?), design, fuel economy, and airplane and automobile design.

The study of aerodynamics brings up the natural paper airplane contest. To add something special to the contest, challenge the students to make a plane for three categories: greatest distance of flight, most accurate (straightest) flight, and longest time in the air flight. Have the students try the scientific method on their projects. Form a hypothesis as to weight, size, design, and shape. Have students test their hypothesis and re-think their airplane designs often, trying to improve upon their original designs. If you give the students some time on this one, you'll get some interesting results. Awards for the winners are located in the back of this book; duplicate as needed.

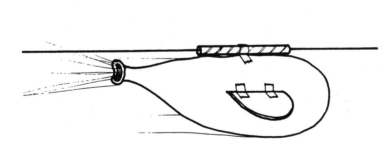

Student Project 19

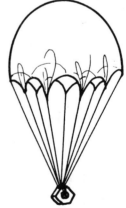

Student Project 20

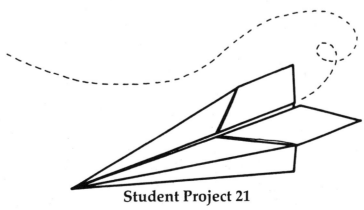

Student Project 21

43

Air Pressure vs. Gravity

Teacher/Student Project 11

The blanket of air that surrounds us extends approximately 100 miles (160 kilometers) above the earth. This ocean of air has weight. Maybe your ears have "popped" as you've gone up a mountain or flown in a plane, or perhaps you have felt the difference in pressure at the top and bottom of a swimming pool? All these feelings were caused by changes in pressure.

At sea level the blanket of air surrounding the earth pushes down with a force of about 15 pounds per square inch (about 1 kilogram per square centimeter). We don't feel these pressures and the tremendous forces and weights because we have equalized the pressure inside our bodies to exactly the pressure outside our bodies. When the outside pressure changes faster than our bodies can change, we can feel the pressure (for example, the ear popping when driving up a mountain). This experiment compares air pressure to the force of gravity.

Materials:

a clean drinking glass
an index card large enough to fit over the mouth of the glass
water

Procedure:

Fill the water glass to the brim with water and place the index card over the top of the glass. It's important that no air bubbles be allowed inside the glass. If you get an air bubble, remove the card, add more water, and replace the card.

Set the glass on your left palm and place your right hand over the card. Quickly, in a fluid motion, turn the glass upside down while still holding with both hands. Do not allow bubbles of air to enter the glass. Slowly remove the hand holding the card. This experiment is best done over a sink during the first few trials.

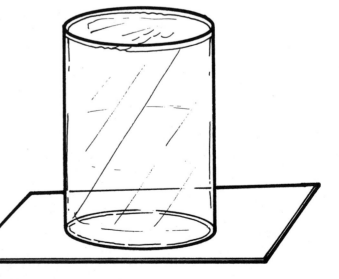

Discussion Question:

Why doesn't the water fall out of the glass?

GA1444

Crushing a Can with Air Pressure

Teacher/Student Project 12

The ocean of air around us is very useful. Without air pressure, a soda straw wouldn't work, a vacuum wouldn't vacuum, an airplane wouldn't fly, and a fan wouldn't blow. To further demonstrate the power of air pressure, we can crush a can with just air pressure.

Materials:

an empty, one-gallon (3.78 liters) duplicating fluid or metal paint thinner can
a hot plate and water

Procedure:

Pour water into a clean, empty one-gallon metal container until the water covers the bottom of the can to a depth of about $1/4$" (approximately .64 cm). Place the can, *without the lid*, on the hot plate. When water boils and steam has been rising from the open container for two to three minutes, quickly and carefully (using a hot pad or towel) lift the can off the hot plate. Quickly screw on the lid until tight and observe the results.

GA1444

Math Project

Calculate the total pounds or kilograms pushing in on the can. Measure the can to determine its size. To determine the area, multiply the length times the width of each side. This measurement will give the area in square units (inches or centimeters). Add together the area of the six sides. Multiply the total area by the pounds (or kilograms) per square unit (inches or centimeters). This number is the total pressure on the can.

length _____ x width _____ = area of top of can x 2 (bottom) = _____

length _____ x width _____ = area of front of can x 2 (back) = _____

length _____ x width _____ = area of side of can x 2 (other side) = _____

Add together the three areas to get total area _____

Multiply by air pressure (14.7 lbs./sq in. or 1 kg/sq cm) _____

Total pressure on can _____

Fill in the blanks in the paragraph below.

The crushed can demonstrates the relationship between heat and pres __ __ __ __. When you saw the __ __ __ __ __ vapor coming from the can, you knew the following:

All the __ __ __ had been forced out of the __ __ __ and the pres__ __ __ __ of the st__ __ __ (water vapor) on the __ __ side was balanced by the pres __ __ __ __ of the air on the outside.

When you removed the can from the __ __ __ plate and screwed on the __ __ __, the can cooled, the pressure in __ __ __ __ the can dropped, a partial vacuum formed inside, and the air __ __ __ __ __ __ __ __ outside started to squ__ __ ze in on the __ __ __.

Water Presssure

Teacher/Student Project 13

Water pressure behaves in much the same way as air pressure. The thicker the "blanket" of water, the greater the pressure. An easy demonstration is accomplished using a can, a nail, and water.

Using a hammer and nail, poke three holes in the can as shown. Fill the can with water and notice the different distances the water "shoots out" from the can.

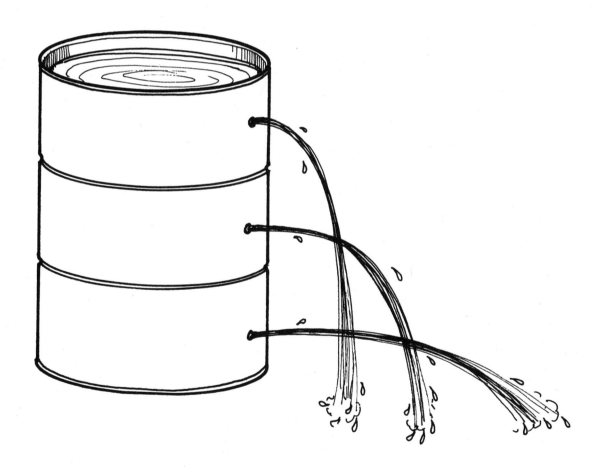

47

Egg in a Bottle

Teacher/Student Project 14

This project demonstrates air pressure in a unique and interesting way. You'll need to find a glass bottle or jar with a mouth slightly smaller than a hard-boiled egg.

Procedure:

1. Put some Vaseline™ or oil on the mouth of the jar to help it to "slide" easier.

2. Roll up about a $1/4$" (.6 cm) sheet of paper, light it with a match, and drop it into the bottle.

3. Quickly place the *peeled* hard-boiled egg over the bottle's mouth.

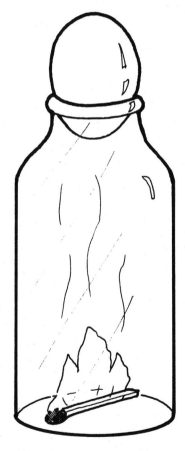

The question arises about getting the egg back out of the bottle. This can be accomplished without breaking the egg or bottle and makes for a good discussion and follow-up. Directions for removing the egg are listed in the answer key.

Hint: Use the same principle to get the egg out that you used to get it in.

Miniature Kites

Student Project 17

Miniature kites are a fun way to demonstrate how moving air can create pressure differences that will fly a kite.

Materials:
    4 plastic soda straws (the stiffer the better)
    cellophane tape
    a plastic bag (grocery type works well)
    a spool of sewing thread
    colored markers

Procedure:
1. Stick one soda straw 2" (6.08 cm) into the end of another straw. Do this for all straws. Tape the two straws together.

2. Tape and tie the two straws with thread so they make the shape of a cross. The cross piece should be about one third of the way down the length of the vertical piece.

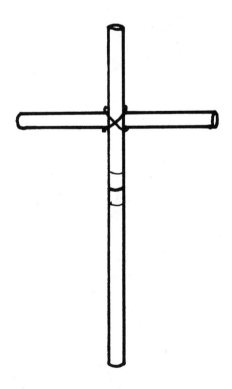

3. Carefully outline the cross with thread. Shallow "slits" cut into the ends of the straws will make the job easier.

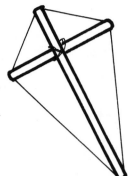

4. Lay the kite frame on a piece of plastic bag and cut around the frame approximately 1" (2.54 cm) larger than the outside of the frame.

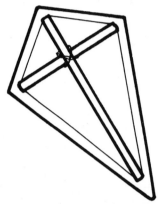

5. Fold 1" (2.54 cm) strip over the string and tape down.

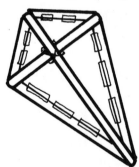

6. Create a backward bow in the kite by tying a thread between the side ends of the kite. The bow string should be about 1" (2.54 cm) from the vertical straw.

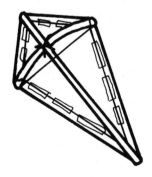

7. Turn the kite over and make a bridle for the front. The bridle is a loose string that ties into the vertical straw halfway between the center and the top, and halfway between the center and the bottom. Cut a small hole in the front of the kite, pass the thread through the skin and tie it to the vertical straw. The bridle should have about 1" (2.54 cm) of slack thread.

8. Attach 2' (61 cm) of approximately 1" (2.54 cm) wide plastic bag for a tail.

9. Tie a thread to the bridle about midway along the bridle string. Some adjustments may need to be made for balance.

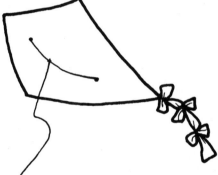

10. Use colored felt-tip pens to personalize your kite and go fly a kite!

Name _____

Date _____

Frictionless Racer

Student Project 18

Building a racer that uses air pressure to overcome friction is a great project. The racer described and illustrated below can be "raced" for speed or distance. Scientifically, air from a balloon is forced through a hole in a board and the resulting air pressure "lifts" the board so it can float on a cushion of air.

Materials:

a $^1/_3$" x 4" x 4" wood scrap (1.91 x 7.62 x 7.62 cm) A piece of plywood or paneling works well.

1 small, wooden thread spool or a 1" x $^3/_4$" doweling (2.54 x 1.91 cm)

white glue

balloon

Procedure:

1. Glue a small wooden thread spool or a 1" x $^3/_4$" (2.54 x 1.91 cm) doweling to the center of your wood scrap. (The bottom of the doweling must be flat.)

2. When dry, drill a $^1/_8$" or $^3/_{16}$" (preferred) hole through the doweling and wooden block.

3. Attach a balloon, inflate and slide on a smooth surface, such as a tabletop.

4. Paint, decorate, and personalize your racer.

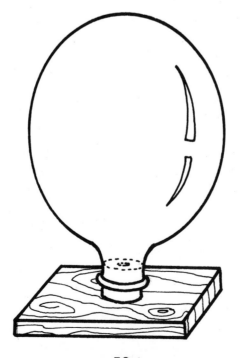

GA1444

Races:

Several rubber bands can be joined together to make a frictionless racer launcher. This will give uniformity on launches. A winning racer is one that will travel the longest distance on a floor. (Floor must be perfectly clean and free of any grit, sand, etc.)

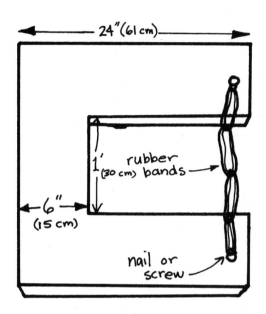

Launcher constructed of $^3/_4$", 2' (1.9 cm, .61 cm) square piece of plywood.

Balloon Rocket Races

Student Project 19

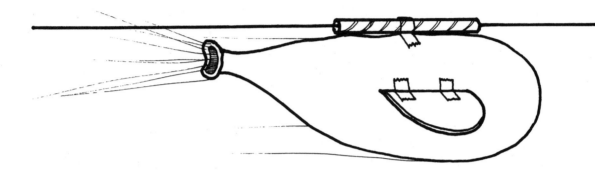

Sir Isaac Newton, a famous English scientist of the 1600's, was the first to discover and write down some of the scientific principles we use today. Newton's third law of motion states that every action has an equal but opposite reaction. This is the physical principle that allows for jet flight today.

Using this principle of action-reaction, develop a balloon racer faster than your competition. You will be able to use any "add ons" you wish as long as you use just one balloon and 30 feet (9.12 m) of string. Using your imagination, develop a hypothesis (an educated guess) about the ways you can speed your balloon down the string. Modifications can be made to the balloon or string and anything goes.

Race Rules:

1. All balloons must travel the same distance. (30 feet [9.12 m] works well.)

2. After the race starts, the balloon may not be touched.

3. The first balloon to the finish line wins.

4. Members may not interfere with other teams.

Good luck and good racing.

> *Edmund Halley, the discoverer of Halley's Comet, persuaded Newton to publish his discoveries.*

Parachutes

Student Project 20

The parachute works on the principle of air resistance. Follow the directions below to build a parachute. Personalize your creation with colored, felt-tip pens.

Materials:
a large plastic grocery or trash bag
string
a weight appropriate for the size of your parachute
masking tape

Procedure:
1. Cut your plastic bag to make the largest piece of plastic possible.

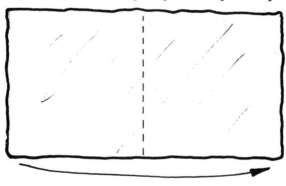

2. Fold in half.

3. Fold in half again.

4. Fold a third time.

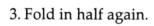

5. Cut on dotted line.

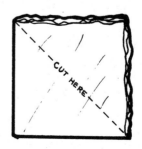

6. Open.

7. Cut four pieces of string, each approximately 2' (.61 m) long.

8. Tape the strings to the plastic as illustrated.

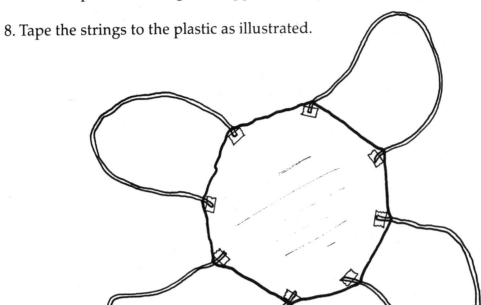

9. Decorate and personalize your parachute.

10. Attach an appropriate weight (small nut or bolt for a small parachute to a heavier item for a larger parachute).

11. Roll up your parachute and toss skyward.

Aerodynamics Contest

Student Project 21

Design your own airplane. Test it. Try different shapes, different forms, different kinds of paper. How about a paper clip for nose weight? Do you have to have it shaped like an "airplane"? As you try various designs and materials, keep a record of your attempts. All airplanes must be constructed of paper (no balsa wood). Glue, tape, paper clips, etc., *are* allowed.

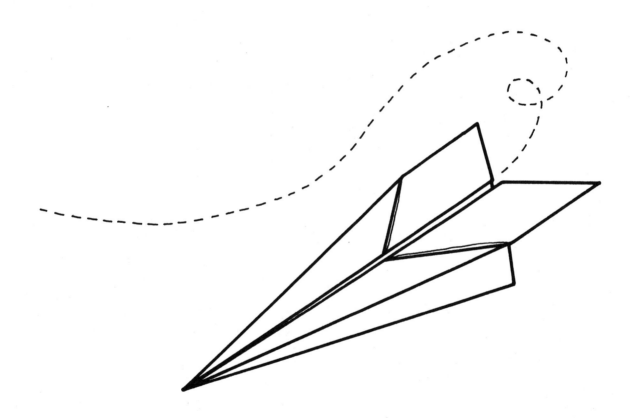

Three categories of winners will be:
1. The device that remains airborne for the longest time
2. The device that travels the greatest distance
3. The device with the most unique design

Orville and Wilbur Wright's first flight went 120 feet (37 meters).

Sound

Sound is all around us. From the screech of fingernails on a chalkboard to the tones of a Beethoven symphony, all sound is the result of vibrations. Sound travels in waves, not unlike those you see when a pebble is tossed into a lake.

Sound travels at different speeds in different mediums. It travels slower in air than wood, steel, or water. The speed with which sound travels through a medium depends on the medium's density, elasticity, and temperature. Sound does not travel in a vacuum. (There is no sound on the moon or in outer space.)

A sound's pitch is determined by how fast the object vibrates. Normally, we can hear frequencies (the number of times it vibrates in a second) from around 20 hertz (vibrations per second) to 20,000 hertz. Some animals, such as dogs and bats, can hear frequencies much higher. To demonstrate sound and its vibrations, several interesting projects may be performed.

If you can get a tuning fork, you can see the fork's vibrations by striking the tuning fork on a cushioned surface (the sole of a shoe works well) and sticking it in a cup of water. The vibrations will splatter the water. The tuning fork can be placed on various objects around the classroom to demonstrate sound amplification.

Two metal spoons or forks tied to strings make a great demonstration. The bell sound the spoons give when struck will amaze the students. Index cards or paper cones can be used to demonstrate how sound can be amplified by increasing the area vibrating. The construction of paper cup telephones will demonstrate the transmission of sound through a string. (Try wire as well.)

Teacher/Student Project 15

Teacher/Student Project 16

Teacher/Student Project 17

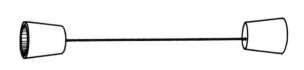

Student Project 22

GA1444

Tuning Forks

Teacher/Student Project 15

A tuning fork can be used to discover some of the hidden qualities of sound. Always strike a tuning fork gently against a rubber object, such as the sole of a shoe. A tuning fork vibrates at a predetermined rate. The speed or frequency of a tuning fork is usually stamped on its handle. A tuning fork's pitch is determined by its frequency. The higher the frequency, the higher the pitch.

After listening to a tuning fork vibrate in the air, place the handle of the tuning fork on various items in the classroom. Note the results.

Place the vibrating "tongs" of a tuning fork in a glass of water. The splattering water shows the tuning fork's vibrations.

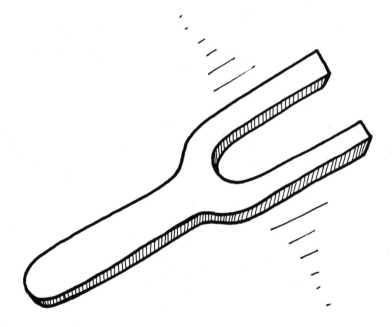

Discussion Questions:
1. Does the pitch change as the tuning fork is placed on various objects? Does the volume change?
2. Why is the sound louder from some objects and not as loud from others?

Bells from Spoons

Teacher/Student Project 16

A spoon can be made to produce a dramatic bell tone. For this project you will need two metal spoons and a piece of string. Tie the spoons to the string so they can strike each other. Wrap the string over your fingertips and place your fingertips in your ears. Move the spoons so they strike each other and you'll hear the spoons sound like bells.

If possible, repeat the project using larger spoons or forks or combinations. Try other objects.

What conclusions can you draw after comparing the sounds generated?

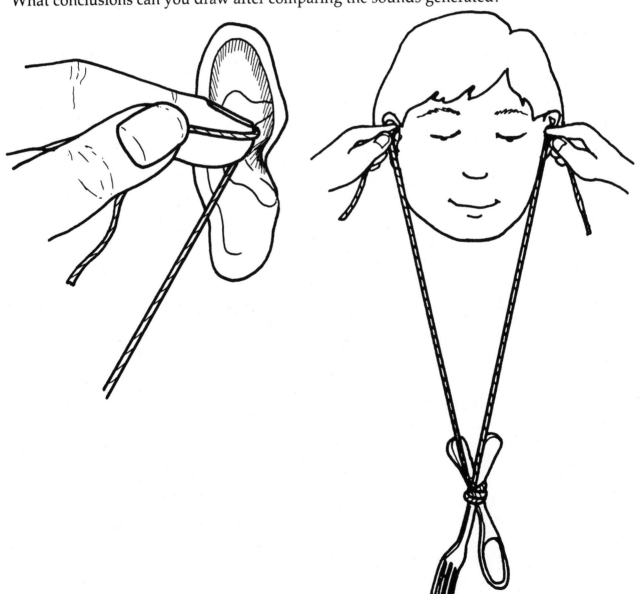

Index Card Speakers

Teacher/Student Project 17

Sound can be amplified by increasing the area from which a sound comes. An interesting project to demonstrate this can be done with an index card, a straight pin, and a record player.

Stick a pin through the corner of an index card and let it rest on an old record. The grooves in the record will cause the pin to vibrate. These vibrations will pass through the pin into the card and cause it to vibrate. The vibrating card will produce sound.

Try shaping the card into a cone and compare the sound generated. Try different shapes of cards and cones and compare the volume of the sounds they generate.

Discussion Question:

Why is the index card speaker not as loud as that of the phonograph speaker?

Name _____

Date _____

Paper Cup Telephones

Student Project 22

Sound is caused by vibrations. Vibrations can be transmitted through the air, through wood, steel, plastic, or even paper and string. To demonstrate how vibrations can travel in a string, you can make paper cup telephones. When you hold a paper or plastic cup over your mouth and speak into it, the bottom (and sides) of the cup will vibrate. If you have stretched a string (very tightly) to another cup, your partner will hear your voice as the vibrations travel down the string and into your partner's cup.

Materials:
   2 paper or plastic cups
   2 paper clips
   a length of string (anywhere from 50′ to 100′ long will work)

Procedure:
   1. Use an "opened" paper clip to make a hole in the bottom of the cup.

   2. Stick the string through the hole and tie the paper clip to it. (This makes it more difficult to pull your cup and string apart.)

   3. Repeat procedure with the other cup.

   4. Stretch your cups apart with the string pulled very taut. Take turns talking on your new telephone.

GA1444

Variations:
- Try substituting wire for the string and compare your results.
- Wax your string with crayon and compare the sounds.
- Compare your modifications with those of your classmates.
- Challenge: Create a partyline with another team of students.

Try these telephone greetings from around the world:

Japan:	"moshi-moshi" (hello)	Israel:	"shalom" (peace)
Mexico:	"bueno" (good day)	Saudi Arabia:	"na' am" (yes)
India:	"hanji" (greetings)	Italy:	"pronto" (ready)
Turkey:	"allo" (hello)	Germany:	"hallo" (hello)

The first telephone message was sent on March 10, 1876, when Alexander Graham Bell spilled some acid on his clothes and called to his assistant in the next room. Bell cried out, "Mr. Watson, come here. I need you."

GA1444

Machines

Machines are devices that do work in an easier, faster, or more accurate way than could be done by hand. While the list of machines is almost endless (a good class project is to list all the machines that you can) most machines consist of one or more of the six basic machines. The lever, the wheel and axle, the pulley, the inclined plane, the wedge, and the screw are considered the six simple machines. The students will be familiar with some aspects of the machines; however, some experimentation may demonstrate these machines' ability to make work easier.

Anyone who has ever used a piece of wood or screwdriver as a lever will verify that force can be increased with its use. A simple pencil experiment performed by pairs easily demonstrates the principle of the lever.

The wheel and axle is familiar to all students. The gears on a multispeed bicycle are examples of how gear size can make work easier. Your classroom pencil sharpener can be used to demonstrate the multiplying force of the wheel and axle.

The pulley (a modified wheel and axle) can be demonstrated in an acceptable manner by a homemade thread spool and clothes hanger pulleys. Multiple pulleys can demonstrate the block and tackle. Equally impressive in demonstrating the multiplying effect of pulleys is a simple experiment using broomsticks and a rope.

The mechanical advantage of an inclined plane can easily be demonstrated with a board, a spring balance and a toy car. Have the students note the difference between the force needed to lift the toy vertically and to pull it up the inclined plane. The wedge is a double-inclined plane and can be demonstrated by making a wedge from a piece of wood, hammering it under a table leg to show how it can lift or separate an object.

The screw is a circular inclined plane. This can be demonstrated by a piece of paper cut into a right triangle and wound around a pencil.

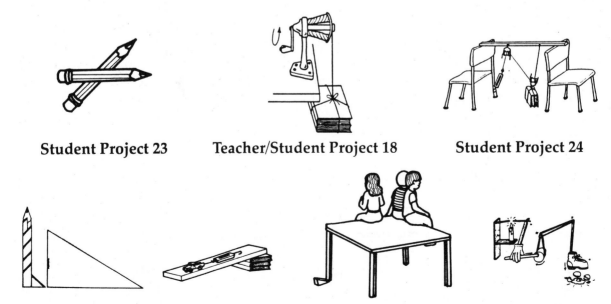

Student Project 23 **Teacher/Student Project 18** **Student Project 24**

Student Project 25 Student Project 26 Teacher/Student Project 19 Student Project 27

GA1444

The Lever

Student Project 23

The lever is perhaps the simplest of all the simple machines. There are three classes of levers. Working together with a partner, you can easily explore the mechanical advantage the lever provides. The lever is considered a machine because it makes work easier. To demonstrate this mechanical advantage, you'll need a partner and two pencils or two pieces of doweling.

Procedure:

| **Figure 1** | **Figure 2** | **Figure 3** |

The three figures above show the relative position of the pencils for the test. Use your finger to hold down one end of the pencil with the force equal to the weight of three to four books. As your partner pushes at the other end of the pencil, have him or her note the ease or difficulty of lifting your finger. Change the position to Figures 2 and 3 and note the change. Reverse jobs and note the change in force necessary to raise your partner's finger.

The three classes of levers are illustrated on the following page.

GA1444

1st Class Lever	**2nd Class Lever**	**3rd Class Lever**

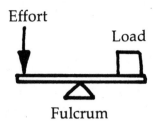
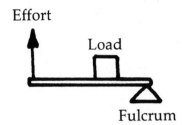
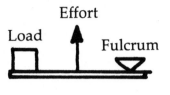

A teeter-totter is a 1st class lever.	A wheelbarrow is a 2nd class lever.	The forearm is a 3rd class lever.

Archimedes said that he could lift the earth if he had a long enough lever and a fulcrum on which to put it.

The Wheel

Teacher/Student Project 18

The wheel is a simple machine. It allows your bike to overcome friction and its gears allow you to increase your force to climb a hill. The pencil sharpener in the classroom can be used to demonstrate the wheel's ability to make work easier. Remove the cover and tie a piece of string to the end as illustrated. Tie several books for weight to the other end of the string and note how easily you can lift the weight.

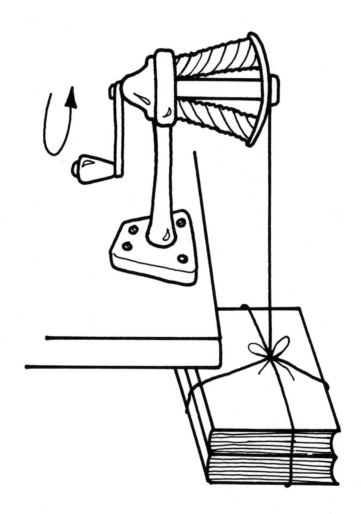

Other examples of the use of a wheel are doorknobs, can openers, gears in a watch, and the blades of a fan. How many others can you name?

Name _____

Date _____

The Pulley

Student Project 24

Building and experimenting with a pulley is the best way to understand how a pulley can multiply force to make work easier. After you have built your pulley, you and a partner can work together to observe how two pulleys can make the work of lifting even easier.

Materials:

    a wire clothes hanger
    an empty thread spool
    pliers, wire cutters
    spring balance

Directions:

1. Cut the clothes hanger so each leg is approximately 8" (20.32 cm) long.
2. Make 90 degree bends in the hanger and thread them through the thread spool.
3. Bend down the ends and adjust so the spool is level and spins smoothly.

Procedure:

1. Use the spring balance to determine the weight of a small book or other object.
2. Tie the string to the book and wrap it over the spool.
3. Use the balance to record how much force it takes to lift the book.
4. Place a ruler between two chairs and assemble two pulleys as illustrated.
5. Record the amount of force now needed to lift the book.
6. Record all your results in the chart on the next page.

68

GA14443

Force needed to lift book
without use of pulley _____ (F_1)

Force needed to lift book
with use of one pulley _____ (F_2) _____ %

Force needed to lift book
using two pulleys _____ (F_3) _____ %

Determine the percent of reduction in force needed to lift the book by using the following formula:

$$\% \text{ of force reduction} = \frac{F_1 - F_2}{F_1} \times 100$$

The Screw

Student Project 25

The screw is an inclined plane arranged in a spiral. Put together two 2" x 4" x 12" (5.08 x 10.16 x 30.48 cm) pieces of wood with a nail and two more 2" x 4" x 12" pieces of wood with a screw. Attempting to get the boards apart with a pry bar will very easily compare the mechanical advantage of a screw over a nail.

To demonstrate that a screw is a circular inclined plane, cut out the figure below. Use crayon or marker to color the edge of the hypotenuse (long side). Start with the end marked *pencil*; slowly wrap the triangle around the pencil. As you do this, the hypotenuse will represent the inclined plane and illustrate a screw.

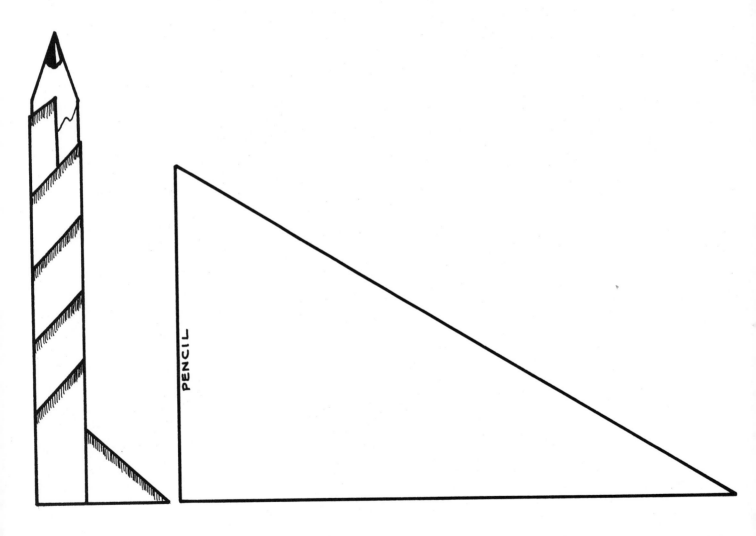

PENCIL

GA1444

The Inclined Plane

Student Project 26

The inclined plane may not seem to be a machine, but it lessens the amount of force needed to lift an object. Attach a spring balance to a toy truck and note the difference between the force needed to lift it vertically and the force needed to pull it up an inclined plane.

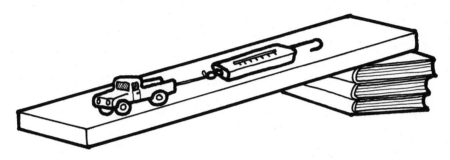

Vary the angle of the inclined plane and record the results. As the incline gets steeper, is the amount of force needed to pull the truck increased or decreased?

Degree of Incline	Amount of Force Needed to Raise the Truck

The Wedge

Teacher/Student Project 19

The screw and wedge are inclined planes that are forced into an object or between two objects. Knives, scissors, nails, pins, and ice picks are all wedges. Cut a wooden wedge from a 2" x 4" (5.08 x 10.16 cm) piece of lumber. Place the tip of the wedge under a table leg. Have three or four students sit on the table and tap the broad end with a hammer. As the wedge is tapped, the table will rise.

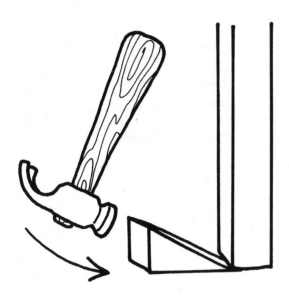

GA1444

The Motion Machine

Student Project 27

Machines come in a variety of sizes, colors, and functions. Most machines create something from either raw materials or assemble materials into a finished product. Also, most machines are composed of moving parts.

Your project is to make a machine that does something. It can strike a match or hit a golf ball, it may lift a shoe or squirt perfume, it can create a lovely sound or squash a bug. Anything goes. Your creativity is being challenged to create a motion machine. It must move and do something. How it moves and what it does are up to you. You will be judged on creativity, originality, neatness, and how well your machine completes its tasks. Anything goes. . .well, almost anything. Nothing dangerous is allowed, but the only other limitation is your imagination.

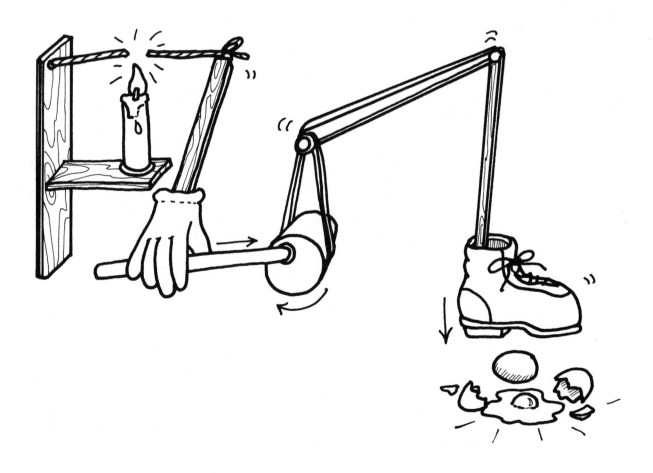

Additional Fun Projects

Some other fun projects have been included. The "freezing flowers" demonstrate ice crystallization at extremely low temperatures. It is one of the most graphic illustrations of science you can perform and, although located at the back of the book, can be a great introduction into a science unit on temperature, crystals, botany, chemistry, or just a "gee whiz" experience for the kids. Notice carefully the precautions because you'll be dealing with some very cold temperatures.

Building straw towers is an interesting and fun method of studying the geometry of construction and the strength of geometric design.

The floating and sinking egg demonstration is a great exercise in studying density. You may wish to have a cotton ball, a marshmallow, a piece of wood, a rock, and a piece of steel to help dramatize the project. A piece of volcanic pumice and a piece of ironwood can also be used (if available) to show a floating rock and sinking piece of wood.

A class bubble day is another great introduction idea. Using the described equipment can make it possible to put a student inside a bubble. The project is nicknamed "monster bubbles" but don't overlook the science of surface tension, chemistry, and the opportunity to compare different bubble mixtures.

Teacher/Student Project 20

Teacher/Student Project 21

Student Project 28

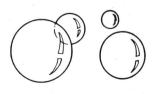

Teacher/Student Project 22

GA1444

Freezing Flowers

Teacher/Student Project 20

Caution:
Because of the very cold temperatures generated by this project, students should be kept back at least five feet (about two meters); protective gloves should be worn as well as protective glasses.

Don't let the caution scare you off of this project. Use care; proceed slowly, and the results will amaze the students.

Materials:
> protective eye covering
> protective hand coverings (garden gloves)
> 1 quart of acetone (available at most paint stores)
> about 5 pounds (2.25 kg) of dry ice (frozen CO_2)
> clean 1 lb. coffee can or metal pot
> tongs (preferably metal or wood)
> assorted flowers, rubber band, small balloon filled with water

Procedure:
Fill can or pot two-thirds full of acetone. Break up and (using tongs) slowly add half-dollar size pieces of dry ice. (It will bubble violently.) Continue adding dry ice until bubbling stops.

Some replacement of acetone may be necessary if the project "boils over" (a misnomer because we're actually cooling the liquid). Using the tongs, grasp the stem of a flower and submerge the blossom into the can. After four or five seconds, the flower can be removed and, although it will look quite normal, the moisture in the petals will have frozen and will shatter like glass when dropped.

Try several flowers, a rubber band (its elasticity is gone when frozen), or a water-filled balloon to make a water ball. The water ball takes a bit longer (thirty seconds). Cut the balloon away from the frozen water ball and let the students pass it around.

The acetone has a very low freezing point, and the temperature of the dry ice, which is about -100°F (about -37.7°C), makes the mixture very cold. The "steam" over the liquid is actually frozen water vapor. The "snow" that forms on the outside of the can is water vapor in the air that freezes when it comes into contact with the ultra cold can.

Dry ice can be obtained at many ice cream stores, some ice houses, and may even be available from the milkman who services your school.

To discard the mixture, allow it to come back to room temperature. You can pour it back into its original container. Add a drop or two of perfume to the mixture, and you have a lifetime supply of fingernail polish remover.

Straw Towers

Student Project 28

The straw towers project is a mixture of construction skills, scientific hypothesis and deduction, and creativity. The task before you is to build a straw structure of maximum height. You may use only the building materials listed below. Your structure must be built without tape or glue and must be freestanding without any attachments to any other objects.

Materials:
    25 soda straws
    20 regular straight pins

Procedure:
    Design and build a straw structure that attains the greatest height possible.

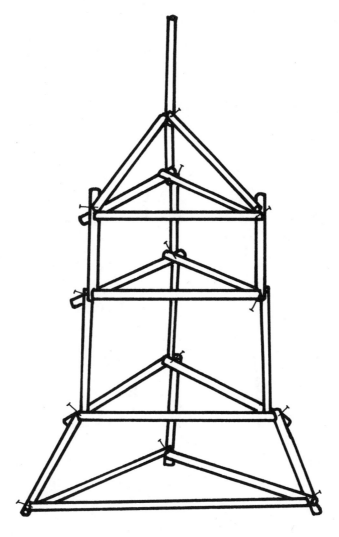

Floating and Sinking Eggs

Teacher/Student Project 21

A project to demonstrate the difference in the density of fresh and salt water is easy to perform.

Place an uncooked egg (shell on) in a glass of warm water. The egg will sink to the bottom. Adding salt (about 20 tablespoons) and stirring will dissolve the salt in the water, changing the water's density which causes the egg to rise. Adding more fresh water will cause the egg to sink once again.

This explains why boats float "higher" in ocean water than when they are in rivers or lakes.

Fresh H$_2$O

Salt H$_2$O

GA1444

Monster Bubbles

Teacher/Student Project 22

Everyone loves bubbles. Try some bendable wire and have the students experiment with different shaped frames. Observe the resulting bubble shapes. Try some 3-D shapes, squares, triangles, squiggles, loops, and figure eights. Predict the shape of the 3-D frame bubbles and compare your results.

Monster bubbles can be created by filling a small plastic swimming pool 2" (5.08 cm) deep with bubble solution and using a Hula-Hoop™. A small plastic wash basin may also be used as a "community bubble pot." Scoop off the foam from the bubble "pool" using your hands.

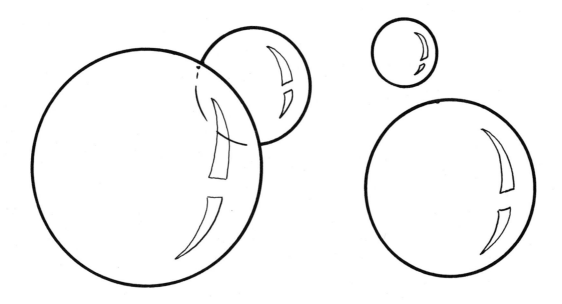

Students can also try clothes hangers, cans and cups with both ends cut out, six-pack soda rings and just about anything with a hole in it to blow bubbles.

Depending on the amount of bubble liquid desired, use about 10 cups (2400 ml) of cold water for every cup of liquid dishwashing soap. Adding three or four tablespoons (45 or 60 ml) of glycerine (optional) may make the bubbles last longer before bursting.

Bubble production is dependent on temperature (low is better), humidity (high is better), and dish soap used. The thicker, clear-type of liquid soap seems to work better than the runny, milky-looking soaps. Bubble blowing is great science, and experimenting to make larger or longer-lasting bubbles is great fun.

GA1444

Possible Research Topics

1. Gravity
2. Air Pressure
3. Force Fields
4. Magnetism
5. Electricity
6. Crystals
7. Chemicals
8. Water
9. Acids and Bases
10. Circuits
11. Computers
12. Kites
13. Aerodynamics
14. Rocketry
15. The Mechanics of Sports
16. Chemistry
17. Sound
18. Music
19. Machines
20. Inventors
21. Communications
22. Alexander Graham Bell
23. Sir Isaac Newton
24. Thomas Edison
25. Patents
26. Light
27. Lasers
28. Colors
29. Heat
30. Molecules
31. Atoms
32. Mining
33. Tools as Machines
34. Uses of Household Chemicals
35. Alfred B. Nobel
36. Nobel Prize
37. Transistor
38. Nuclear Power
39. Edwin Armstrong
40. George Washington Carver
41. Samuel Cole
42. John Deere
43. Philo T. Farnsworth
44. Charles Goodyear
45. Henry Ford
46. George Westinghouse
47. Rudolf Diesel
48. Leonardo da Vinci

GA1444

Word Search

Find and circle the words listed below.

air	pressure	sound	frequency
invention	Newton	motor	saturated
atom	speed	laser	electricity
molecule	force	color	crystal
machine	time	Nobel	
chemical	friction	vibration	
electron	light	aerodynamics	

S	O	U	N	D	M	O	T	O	R	O	B	N	V	C	G	E	L
U	P	P	U	O	W	N	F	R	I	C	T	I	O	N	A	T	A
I	S	A	T	U	R	A	T	E	D	G	E	X	T	N	Y	H	S
E	V	F	R	E	Q	U	E	N	C	Y	R	S	P	E	E	D	E
W	E	B	E	H	P	R	E	S	S	U	R	E	R	W	T	V	R
H	L	D	R	T	E	C	H	E	M	I	C	A	L	T	E	I	B
E	E	R	A	I	Q	R	R	L	O	S	O	P	B	O	C	B	N
A	C	G	B	N	W	Y	X	E	L	Y	L	Z	B	N	K	R	O
E	T	W	A	V	R	S	M	C	E	P	O	M	A	P	M	A	B
E	R	A	F	E	N	T	X	T	C	R	R	A	T	O	M	T	E
A	I	R	O	N	B	A	T	R	U	Q	G	C	H	T	J	I	L
R	C	G	R	T	N	L	I	O	L	I	G	H	T	N	F	O	L
S	I	F	C	I	O	O	M	N	E	K	L	I	E	R	A	N	K
D	T	A	E	O	T	A	E	R	O	D	Y	N	A	M	I	C	S
O	Y	T	T	N	R	U	A	S	L	D	J	E	C	P	X	R	V

Awards

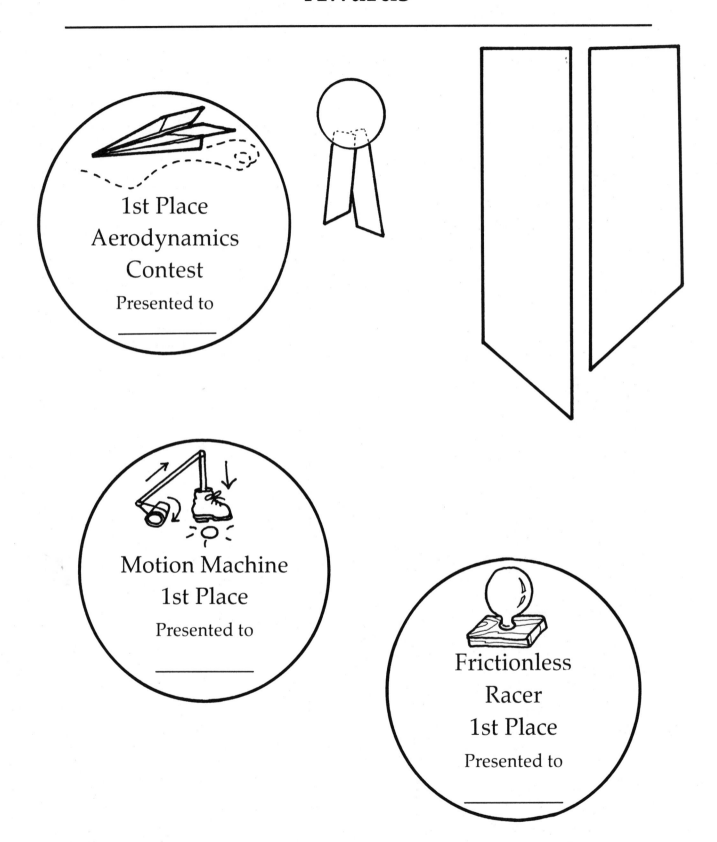

1st Place
Aerodynamics
Contest
Presented to
_____

Motion Machine
1st Place
Presented to
_____

Frictionless
Racer
1st Place
Presented to
_____

Awards

Light Reflection
Relay Race
1st Place

Presented to

_____

Balloon Rocket
Race
1st Place

Presented to

_____

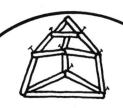

Straw Towers
1st Place

Presented to

_____

GA1444

AWARD

Presented to

_____

for
Participation in

_____

signed_____
date_____

GA1444

Certificate
of Merit

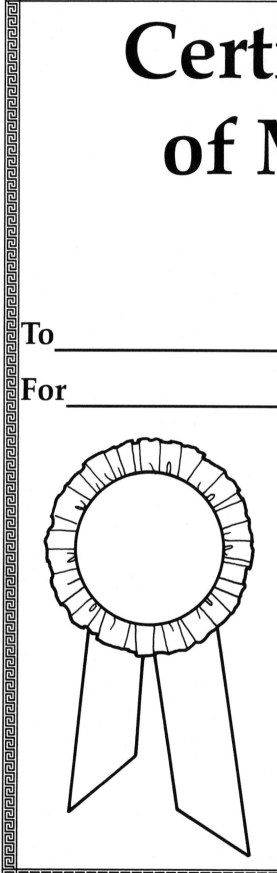

To_____

For_____

_____
signed

_____
date

Graph Paper

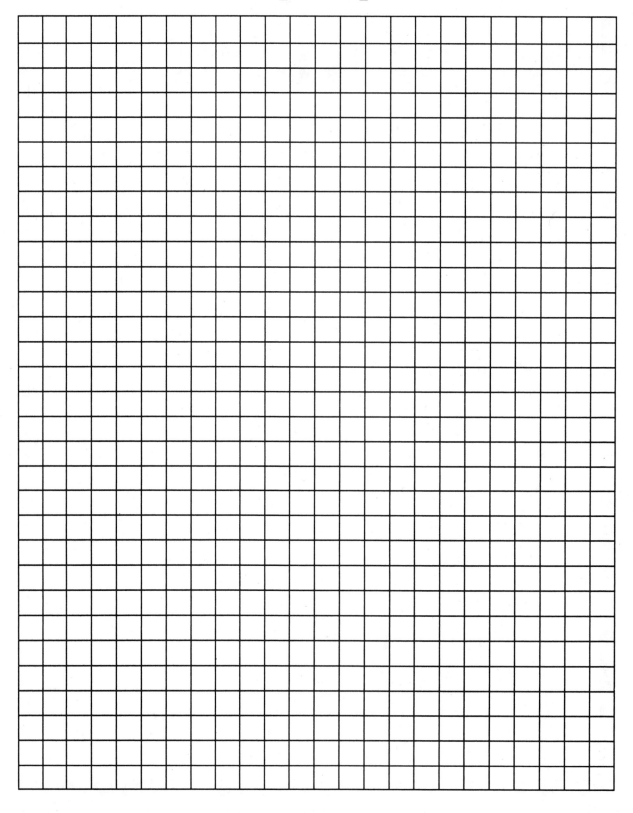

Dear Parents,

Our class is currently studying science, and we are in need of a number of materials. If it is possible, could you contribute some of the necessary items listed below? Your help with your child's projects is appreciated. Please take this opportunity to discuss with your child the science projects we are completing at school. Thank you for your support.

Sincerely,

We need the following items:

_____

_____

_____

_____

_____

_____

_____

_____

GA1444

Science Supply Companies

Carolina Biological Supply Company
2700 York Road
Burlington, NC 27215
(800) 334-5551

Central Scientific Co.
11222 Melrose Ave.
Franklin Park, IL 60131

Delta Education
P.O. Box 950
Hudson, NH 03051-9924
(800) 442-5444

Edmund Scientific Co.
101 E. Glouster Pike
Barrington, NJ 08007

Este Industries (Rocketry)
Dept. 1695
Penrose, CA 81240

Fisher Scientific Company
Educational Materials Div.
4901 W. LeMoyne St.
Chicago, IL 60651

FSC Educational Inc.
905 Hickory Lane
P.O. Box 8101
Mansfield, OH 44901-8101
(419) 589-1900

NASCO
901 Janesville Ave.
Ft. Atkinson, WI 53538

NASCO West
P.O. Box 3837
Modesto, CA 95352
(209) 529-5957

Turtox, Inc.
5000 W. 128th Place
Alsip, IL 60658

Wards Natural Science
5100 W. Henrietta Rd.
P.O. Box 92912
Rochester, NY 14692

Other Science-Related Addresses

The Good Apple Newspaper
Good Apple
1204 Buchanan St., Box 299
Carthage, IL 62321-0299

National Aeronautic and Space
    Administration (NASA)
Educational Branch
Washington, D.C. 20546

National Geographic Society
17th and M Streets NW
Washington, D.C. 20036

National Science Teachers Assoc.
1742 Connecticut Ave. NW
Washington, D.C. 20009

National Wildlife Federation
1412 16th St. NW
Washington, D.C. 20036

Every effort has been made, at the time of publication, to insure the accuracy of the information included in this book. We cannot guarantee, however, that the agencies and organizations we have mentioned will continue to operate or to maintain these current locations indefinitely.

GA1444

Physical Science Test

Write *true* or *false* in front of each statement.

1. _____ Everything that can be touched is composed of atoms.

2. _____ Oxygen, gold, and protons are composed of atoms.

3. _____ Baking soda reacts with vinegar to make oxygen gas.

4. _____ Quartz is a crystal.

5. _____ A cold solution will dissolve more material than a hot one.

6. _____ Litmus paper can be used to test for an acid or a base.

7. _____ An iron nail is a magnetic object.

8. _____ Electricity can be used to create a magnetic field.

9. _____ The angle at which light strikes a mirror is half the angle at which the beam is reflected.

10. _____ White light is composed of all the colors of the rainbow.

11. _____ Air has weight.

12. _____ The speed (frequency) at which an object vibrates determines the pitch.

13. _____ Sound is caused by vibration.

14. _____ The six simple machines are levers, computers, pulleys, motors, wedges, and screws.

15. _____ Dry ice is frozen CO_2.

Answer Key

Dancing Macaroni, page 9
CO_2 gas attaches to the macaroni causing it to rise.

Magnetic Objects, page 21
Magnetic objects: nail, paper clip

Air Pressure vs. Gravity, page 44
The card stays up because the force of the air pressure pushing up on the card is greater than the force of gravity pulling down on the water.

Crushing a Can with Air Pressure, page 46
pressure, water, air, can, pressure, steam, inside, pressure, hot, lid, inside, pressure, squeeze, can

Egg in a Bottle, page 48
To get the egg out of the bottle, invert the bottle and seal the lip of the bottle with your mouth. Blow hard inside the bottle and the egg will "pop" out.

Tuning Forks, page 59
The pitch does not change, just the volume; some objects transmit more sound while others absorb sound.

Index Card Speakers, page 61
The phonograph uses an electronic amplifier to increase sound.

Physical Science Test, page 89

1. T	9. F
2. F	10. T
3. F	11. T
4. T	12. T
5. F	13. T
6. T	14. F
7. F	15. T
8. T	

Word Search, page 81

S	O	U	N	D	M	O	T	O	R	O	B	N	V	C	G	E	L
U	P	P	U	O	W	N	F	R	I	C	T	I	O	N	A	T	A
I	S	A	T	U	R	A	T	E	D	G	E	X	T	N	Y	H	S
E	V	F	R	E	Q	U	E	N	C	Y	R	S	P	E	E	D	E
W	E	B	E	H	P	R	E	S	S	U	R	E	R	W	T	V	R
H	L	D	R	T	E	C	H	E	M	I	C	A	L	T	E	I	B
E	E	R	A	I	Q	R	R	L	O	S	O	P	B	O	C	B	N
A	C	G	B	N	W	Y	X	E	L	Y	L	Z	B	N	K	R	O
E	T	W	A	V	R	S	M	C	E	P	O	M	A	P	M	A	B
E	R	A	F	E	N	T	X	T	C	R	R	A	T	O	M	T	E
A	I	R	O	N	B	A	T	R	U	Q	G	C	H	T	J	I	L
R	C	G	R	T	N	L	I	O	L	I	G	H	T	N	F	O	L
S	I	F	C	I	O	O	M	N	E	K	L	I	E	R	A	N	K
D	T	A	E	O	T	A	E	R	O	D	Y	N	A	M	I	C	S
O	Y	T	T	N	R	U	A	S	L	D	J	E	C	P	X	R	V